PRESENCE

Recognizing the Divine
in Your Everyday Life

Stephanie,
Holding you in
the Light
with care.
Mary

Mary G. Jackson, MEd, MS, LCPC
Pastoral Counselor

Printed in the United States of America

Published in Hellertown, PA

Cover design by Kristen Williams

Cover photo by Mary G. Jackson

Library of Congress information available upon request.

ISBN 978-1-952481-53-6

2 4 6 8 10 9 7 5 3 1 paperback

Bright
COMMUNICATIONS

BrightCommunications.net

Contents

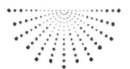

Introduction

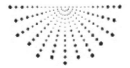

We will explore how to look for something that has always been there, but perhaps you haven't noticed before.
(Photo by Robert Els for Quechua Benefit)

Thy his book is about you and your spiritual journey. It's about the search for the connection between you as the beloved creation of the Divine and the mystery hidden in plain sight right here on Earth, right now.

This book is also about me and my journey that I will share, hopefully offering you deeper understanding.

Together, we will explore new ways to ignite your awareness. You may discover the inspiration that will form the authentic substance of your own personal spiritual journey.

PRESENCE will offer you fresh ideas to consider, unique methods to explore, and profound ways to live your life fully aware of your ever-present spiritual journey. You may then take your new perspective into your present and future life, continually enriching your spiritual journey.

There will be a variety of ways PRESENCE will guide your discovery. We will explore how the Divine shows itself in our lives, and how our everyday lives are filled with that presence. We will discover the Divine in things that are delightful in our lives, when we suffer and fail and have to try again, and when our plans unfold effortlessly or come to an abrupt standstill.

PRESENCE will take you into the world of words and story as we seek to unravel the amazing symbolism in language.

You might discover that some of the most important experiences that you have recalled all your life have a deeper, more spiritual meaning than you could imagine. PRESENCE will open that mystery for you and help you explore your own journey.

Who is PRESENCE for? It is for both Christians and non-Christians. More importantly, it is for you if you are a seeker of spiritual enlightenment. PRESENCE is for those who love their faith but who have had that gut feeling that there could be more. It is for those who doubt their faith but are still open to seek more. It connects your regular, everyday life with the Divine.

My Journey

You might be curious about who wrote this book. There is a story behind how I came to be a seeker, observer, learner, counselor, teacher, and now author. First, I'll share my credentials and work experience, as those sometimes speak to a substantial level of expertise. Then I would like you to get to know me by becoming aware of my journey from life and religion into spirituality.

I am a Licensed Clinical Professional Counselor (LCPC) in private practice and a graduate of Loyola College of Maryland's School of Pastoral Counseling. I hold two master's degrees, the first studying educational psychology and the second a master's in science in counseling, followed by a certificate in advanced study (a post-master's study) in pastoral counseling. My undergraduate study was as an English major, specializing in 17th Century poetry and prose.

I started my work life moving from clinical dental assisting to becoming an Assistant Professor in the Health Sciences Center at the University of Louisville. I shifted into Fortune 500 corporate life as a writer of executive and management development training in the Human Resource Development department of Marriott Corporation, and eventually for multiple clients in my own consulting practice. My move to become a licensed counselor came at midlife.

Now I'll share my journey that wove religious and life experience with a constant sense of seeking. But don't anticipate some amazing transcendent or saintly reveal. My story describes how even a modest spiritual path can lead to life fulfillment.

When I was in the third grade, my parents drove me to church on Sundays, dropped me off, and went back home so my mother could make her Sunday fried chicken, and my father could work on the project of the moment in his basement workshop. I went to church choir and Sunday School at St. Columbus Episcopal Church in a modest

6

neighborhood in Washington, D.C. I was confirmed there, got little from it, but I sensed there was something there, and I was searching.

After abandoning religion in junior high and high school, I went back to church in my twenties, again drawn to choir. This time I attended All Souls Episcopal, dubbed by my irreverent choir friends and me as "Old Souls by the Zoo" as the church was near the National Zoo on Connecticut Avenue in northwest Washington, D.C. The congregation was old, and the minister was old—and dull. The choir, however, was really excellent and full of young adult energy. Again, I had a feeling there was something there, but it was not even close to being obvious to me.

In my thirties, I had a great job designing executive and management training with Marriott Corporation with lots of perks. I could take just about any kind of training I wanted anywhere in the country, and I did. These were no ordinary seminars. Even fairly straightforward business titles offered mindfulness and spirituality without using those exact words.

I delved into Human Interaction Labs at the American University-based National Training Lab (NTL) to experience deep personal discovery in myself and in others. I met Charley Tack, a work colleague, who was a seeker if ever there was one. He talked to me about spirituality every day. I had no church then, but I realized I was on a spiritual odyssey.

In my forties, I adopted two babies from Peru, and I thought I had to find a church for their spiritual development. My search took me to a total of 13 churches of the Protestant choices you have all heard of. I didn't like any of them. I recalled Charley saying to me, "You should try the Quakers."

7

I attended my first Quaker Meeting. And I found my spiritual home there immediately. I loved it.

Being a Quaker is both hard and easy. Quakers experience silence as an opportunity to reflect on their inward connection to the Divine. They base this practice on the Bible instruction from Psalm 46:10, "Be Still and Know that I am God." This was the key that opened my door to contemplative prayer. There was little religious creed, but there were powerful messages expressed through well-used sayings and symbols that spoke to my spiritual truth long felt.

The Light (always capital L) is the symbol for God/Divine/ Christ Spirit, and when praying for you, Quakers "hold you in the Light." Their shared view of religion, which is actually open to much variation, is summed up by the phrase, "That of God in Everyone." That phrase was the foundation that led them to be abolitionists, help prisoners, embrace a peace testimony, be conscientious objectors, and in recent times be welcoming of LGBTQ+ and anti-racism involvement. To acknowledge that the Divine encourages forward direction and movement, Quakers speak of "Way opening." Most wonderfully, because the formal name of Quakers is The Religious Society of Friends, Quakers call each other "Friend" (always capital F).

In recent years, being geographically far from a Quaker Meeting and wanting to cultivate a local church, I became a member of St. Paul's United Church of Christ in Westminster, Maryland. I have taken on many leadership roles in that church, which is known far and wide as a progressive Christian church.

My spiritual journey continues with writing this book and with opening myself to whatever is forthcoming.

8

As you journey through this writing, I hope you will be amazed at how the Divine speaks to you and shows its presence to you in your everyday life.
(Photo by Robert Els for Quechua Benefit)

PRESENCE *Recognizing the Divine in Your Everyday Life*

How to Get the Best from This Book (and Yourself)

First, be prepared to open your heart, mind, and soul to discovery. That means to first embrace an intriguing or new awareness. Then discover what might be clues and question your understanding. Accept what seems to fit, hold that which is possible in a place that may flourish, and reject that which doesn't feel right. Not everything will feel like the right thing or be the right time on your journey.

The story of our lives is unique to each of us and gives instruction for us to grow in understanding, wisdom, and enjoyment of our human time. I hope you will consider that your life story may have been guided by the Divine just as the stories of God's presence and guidance are told in the Bible. The first concept in PRESENCE is *God is a mystery.* As our starting point, that gives you permission to ask many questions that only you can answer, and your answers may grow as you grow on your journey.

My upbringing was in the Protestant religion, which uses the Bible as its foundational literature and identified "word of God." I consider myself ecumenical, but I don't have firsthand experience being raised in other religions. I am a cisgender woman (pronoun preference is she/her), with racial and European culture and lifelong USA citizenship. Like you, I am at ease in my own culture and have unavoidable blindsides in any other culture. I do my very best to be aware of and inclusive to you as a unique and precious individual. If I stumble into a place that in any way "others" you, I will first ask for your understanding of my naiveté and/or ignorance, and I will address it immediately both with you personally and in any

10

correction that can be made for future printings of
PRESENCE.

Because my professional experience has included being a workshop trainer and currently a counselor, I feel most like myself when I engage new ideas as a shared, personal connection with participants who are with me as the reader. Sometimes, I will speak to you directly, as if we were in the same physical space. Other times, I will be moved to connect us, for I envision us on this quest together. Whether I reach out calling to *you* or join you in this by using the word *we,* I hope you will feel our connection as you navigate through PRESENCE.

It is bold to write about God, as if I, or anyone, has an answer, or worse yet, "the" answer. The core of this book is not answers, but questions. As we ask many of the questions presented in the following pages, there are some ways to make the experience of reading this more meaningful.

Just using the word *God* can carry great weight for each of us. In this book, I use a number of words meaning God, including "the Divine," "Spirit," "Light," "the Spirit which passes through all things," "Wholeness," and "Oneness." I will avoid assigning masculine or feminine gender and using corresponding pronouns whenever possible. I welcome you to use a choice that is comfortable for you and translate any uncomfortable identifying word to one that works for you. The most important thing is not to get triggered by or hung up on a word that might distract you from the joy of discovery.

As you journey through this writing, I hope you will be amazed at how the Divine speaks to you and shows its presence to you in your everyday life. I ask you to be like a dry sponge placed gently in a bowl of clear water. As you soak up

11

this abundance, squeeze lightly from time to time to rid yourself of the excess while retaining what is absorbed deeply. If you approach this book and your own journey as if you are already closed, you will miss the opportunity to soak up all the new ideas presented here. Be open, search, and accept, or at least ponder something that moves you. Then reject what doesn't work for you, modify what stimulates your search, and soar with what inspires.

Contact me at presenceeveryday@yahoo.com.

The children in the photos are from the charity-run school Casa Chapi, in the remote highlands of Peru.

Photos and Charity Connection

I am deeply grateful for the sweet photos that you will find in these pages. They are mostly of the young children from the school *Casa Chapi* in the highlands of Peru. The charity

12

Quechua Benefit (www.quechuabenefit.org) has donated them to PRESENCE.

Appreciation and Acknowledgments

Barry Morley

Though there have been many spiritual awakenings in my life, none has been so profound, nor so directly tied to the writing of PRESENCE than the connection with the weighty Quaker Barry Morley. Before his untimely death in 2000, he shared the story of his lifelong spiritual journey, brilliant teachings, and unique perspective with me, which are revealed in this book, especially in Part II.

He wrote a never-published work entitled *The Language of God,* which forms the premise of this book. In 1989, I began as a student, then facilitator, of Barry's weekend retreats called *Inward Bound,* held in a peaceful Quaker camp nestled in the Catoctin Mountains of Maryland. That experience deepened when transforming his work into workshops based on Barry Morley's creative imagination.

For the latter half of my life, I have embraced his *Language of God* as a filter to make sense of my own spiritual path. If I could, I would acknowledge him on every page of this book. And I would lay PRESENCE humbly and gratefully at his feet.

My Editors, Devoted Friends, and Family

My thanks go to Yuri Plowden, who, 14 years after Barry's death, dreamt a dream that sparked our early collaborations presenting our workshops based on his work. Here is how Yuri told me of that dream:

13

Barry and you were with me in a pool of light within the darkness in the lodge at Camp Catoctin. Barry turned to me and said, 'It's all about the journey, Yuri. Look at this experience as a Spiritual journey.'

I am grateful to Pastor Marty Kuchma of St. Paul's United Church of Christ in Westminster, Maryland, who gave me free rein to conduct my first classes that motivated me to write my first draft of PRESENCE.

I appreciate the help of my first editorial team: Yuri Plowden, who attended Barry Morley seminars with me for years; Roban Kubic, with whom I have weekly conversations about spiritual questions; Sarah Ramsland, who is the smartest spiritual seeker I know; Marty Kuchma, whose depth of love and fairness is a stabilizing gift; and Nick Wood, who edits for a profession and leads Bible study in his church. Most recently, thank you to my publisher, Jennifer Bright of Bright Communications LLC, who gave the gift of encouragement when most needed.

My pilot participants, Giancarlo Libertino, Renee Fink, and Jane Dennis, were all patient, loyal, questioning, and fun to teach. Thank you to the St. Paul's UCC Seekers class members, who challenge everything, every Sunday, in our adult education class and keep me on my spiritual toes.

Of course, heartfelt thanks to my daughters, Joanna and Ruthie; my grandson, Christian; and my boyfriend, Rob, who have all shown immense patience with my hours of writing.

PART I

ENCOUNTERING DIVINE PRESENCE

Chapter 1
Looking for Something

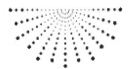

The beach can be enlightening. This day was no different, with a calm breeze, the lapping of bay waves, and still-warm sand. As summer and fall struggled to decide what temperature it should be, and with only a few people to be seen, I walked slowly at the water's edge that morning with my beloved shaggy terrier, Pixie, running ahead. Someone in the distance, who was slower than I, greeted Pixie, who had nosed her way into the solo walk of the stranger.

The woman, about 40ish and pretty, had that beachy casual style of not needing to care about looks. She turned as I attempted to keep my dog from being a nuisance. All was clearly in good stead when we made the expected greeting as two people on a morning beach walk often do, with smiles and a sharing of how lovely all of it was.

She carried a plastic bag with her, partially filled with something I couldn't see, and she clearly was searching for something in the sand. She told me that about a year before, after many years of strolling on this beach, she had found the handle to a trunk or drawer that was intriguing in its age and

16

look, and she had taken it to the local museum for identification. She learned that the *Maria Johanna*, a Dutch merchant ship, had sunk not far into the bay sometime in the 1700s. For centuries, no one remembered it being there. Then, a few decades ago, a boat began dredging the area. Its heavy digging device literally shattered the *Maria Johanna*, unintentionally destroying what had previously lain sleeping and untouched. Glass windows were smashed, and the cargo of liquor bottles was destroyed.

Now, after many years, glass fragments still wash up on shore, particularly when a low tide leaves the path of shells, stones, and sea animal remains in wavy lines that parallel the water's edge. The broken glass, now smooth for the bathing of the waves and sand, washes up with the rest of nature.

Having found the handle, and learning of this story from the local museum, the beachcomber began a search for something that had been there all along, the glass pieces from the bottles and windows, but until now had not been in her awareness. She showed me how to recognize them on the sand, how they proved to be glass when holding them up to the light of the sun, and how to tell the difference between the window glass and the bottle glass.

"I come to the shore now about three times a week and continue to search for the glass," she said showing me the plastic grocery bag with that day's found pieces in it. "I have thousands of pieces I've collected. It is my passion to collect these. It still amazes me that something that has been here my whole life just became present in my life last year, and now I see it easily, and it gives me such joy and purpose to find it."

This collector learned to recognize the glass treasures from

17

The beach can be enlightening.
(Photo by M. Jackson)

the sea through her newfound awareness and focus, as well as her new knowledge, and in this pursuit she found a sense of purpose.

Each time the collector visits the beach, she brings a second bag to collect trash left on the beach to keep it clean. That simple act, so easy to add to her passion of glass collecting, protects the birds and other marine life that might mistake plastic for food.

We walked together for a while as I looked at the glass pieces she collected that day and I learned how to recognize them. After a while, I felt it was time to part, so Pixie and I turned around toward the direction from which we had come. The woman and I spoke pleasant goodbyes and shared smiles before I stopped and turned back. I felt that I should have asked her name, but somehow it didn't happen, and I felt the loss of a missed opportunity.

Recognizing the Divine in everyday life takes awareness, focus, purpose, and knowledge of a language that expands beyond words.
(Photo by Robert Els for Quechua Benefit)

Within just a minute, as I walked back, I passed another person, and again, introduced by Pixie's greeting, we began to have idle chat. Having missed the opportunity to ask my glass collector her name, I made sure I wouldn't do that again, and when I asked this second person what her name was, she responded, "Mary." I was surprised to hear my own name, Mary, spoken aloud.

As I later reflected on that morning, I became increasingly aware of the deeper meaning in my walk. I had traveled to the beach to begin the writing of this book. I decided to take a walk on the beach before starting chapter 1, page 1. How present of the Divine to have me come face-to-face with a living metaphor that would become the beginning. The beachcomber's story of searching was an example of looking for something that had always been there, but not recognized. That she was there, that we met and spoke, make the event more profound than a casual and easily forgotten encounter. Even the details of the encounter had significance.

19

Further along in this book, we will uncover symbols that alert us to God's presence. Some people view the sea as a symbol of the mind of God, and the ship can represent the life journey we are on. When I failed to ask for the name of the first person I met in the morning, I asked the second, and it was the same name as mine. I wonder, was God calling me by name to be aware of the companionship and will of the Divine as I was about to begin my writing?

I am not always sure of the meaning of experiences like these. Like the Divine itself, they are a mystery, which can mean more than one thing; however, I am confident that the surfacing of symbols, metaphors, coincidences, and mysterious occurrences is a spiritual message from God saying, "Pay attention! I am PRESENT!" If we accept that God is present all the time, and that it is *we* who are absent, we can become more aware of that presence.

I would like you to open yourself up to the possibility that just as God spoke to people as recorded in the Bible, God may be speaking to us in the ways that words, concepts, events, and our spiritual journeys lie in front of us in abundance. If we can recognize when that communication reaches us, we can be connected to the Spirit and follow the divine message to support and guide us on our life path. Recognizing the Divine in everyday life takes awareness, focus, purpose, and knowledge of a language that expands beyond words.

Take some time to consider what makes you lose the ability to be aware, and what brings you to a keen sense of awareness. What is on your personal list of distractions? Do you fight your way through the fog of multitasking, overcommitment, exhaustion, urgent interruptions, getting bogged down in low

20

priorities, or not prioritizing at all? Consider what happens when, just for a short time, you switch on your awareness.

Imagine, for example, that you are sitting on the corner of a busy street and mindlessly watching the cars go by. Hundreds may go by without your ever really noticing any of them. However, when a friend calls while you are sitting there and makes plans to pick you up in a few minutes in a red car, you begin to focus on red cars. There are many. As the time grows shorter, there seem to be even more red cars. Maybe you start asking yourself if maroon could be red, so you start noticing that color, too. Soon tomato red, orange red, brownish red, and more are on your radar. Now you are seeing red cars all over the place! Would you like the presence of the Divine to be like that in your life, where you see the Divine everywhere, just because you started noticing?

Noticing what is in front of you is not always so easy. Have you ever played *Where's Waldo?* In a picture with scores of small images, a simple drawing of a man named Waldo hides in plain sight. Your task is to find Waldo. It can take a long time, it can be frustrating, and you may even give up. How is that like your experience of seeking to find God every day? Maybe we can learn from looking for Waldo.

There are widely publicized techniques to increase one's effectiveness to find Waldo quickly. Among them is to spend some time looking at a picture of Waldo all by himself before starting the hunt. The idea is, if your brain can get used to the image of him, once you shift your eyes to the complex drawing in which he is hiding, you can pick up the image more quickly.

Another technique is to anticipate where on the page there is the greatest likelihood he will show up. Some Waldo sleuths have mapped out by computer all the previous places he has

21

been to show a pattern. Using that information, you may narrow your search to certain areas of the page to give you greater speed in your discovery. There are also visual patterns that may increase your proficiency. Looking at the stories that are depicted within the drawing can give you clues.

Let's look at what it takes to begin recognizing the Divine in your everyday life. First, what are you looking for? What do you expect to see? It would be nice if God were easily recognized as the old stereotype of a large man with wavy white hair and a beard, with a deep melodic voice, wearing a robe, and sitting on a cloud above. Like Waldo, this God could be found hiding in plain sight.

In this book, we are going to consider some concepts that are like building blocks explaining the groundwork of spiritual understanding. They don't demand that you believe them, but they have been very helpful to consider along my path, and I offer them to you to mull over throughout the book. Let's look at the first two.

The first concept is *God is a mystery.* It isn't as easy finding God as it is spotting Waldo. We want to explore recognizing the Divine as it relates just to you. The second concept is *The Divine will appear to you in ways that only you recognize.*

Although you call a number of people in your life friends, consider the uniqueness of each relationship. You may prefer one friend to talk with, another to have adventures with, one who is the best to be with when you are sad, and another who is your choice when you are happy and want to celebrate. You may share an interest with one and prefer to share your deepest feelings with another. They are all friends, and they are all in your inner circle.

22

Your neighbor has friends, too. Probably they are different people than those you have in your life, but they likely connect with your neighbor in a similar way as your friends connect with you. The concept that *the Divine will appear to you in ways that only you recognize* is similar to how only you recognize your friends and those special connections that have meaning only to you.

Your very best friend may be totally unimportant or unknown to your neighbor. God's Spirit is in relationship with you in a unique and singular way. Just like you know your best friends like no one else knows them, you can know God in ways that only you recognize. It may not be as easy as finding Waldo on a printed page, but there are questions you can begin asking: How do I know when Spirit is present? How and when has God been present in my life? Even if it is a mystery, how do I know when I recognize the Divine? What name(s) do I use to call the God of my understanding? Focusing takes concentration, practice, and a different way of looking at things.

On a trip to the Grand Canyon, a spiritual place for many, I arrived by airplane at the Phoenix, Arizona, airport. My friend told me we would have to rent a truck to get our gear to the campsite we had reserved because my friend's truck wasn't working.

On the way to the campsite, it started to rain, and we discovered that the rental truck's windshield wipers didn't work. We had to keep going because we needed to get to our destination before dark fell. My friend didn't want to drive with the rain causing an almost impossible obscuring of our view of the road, so I took the wheel to give it a try.

Knowing how important it was for us to get to our camp, without any plan or experience, I found myself focusing not on the drops of rain on the windshield, but *between* the drops. I forced myself to look at the road through the clear spaces. After a while, to my surprise, it became almost normal to see the road clearly ahead. My friend was amazed that it was so easy for me and remarked about how different a perception it was to choose to look not at the obstacle, in this case the raindrops, but through or beyond it.

It matters what you focus on. It might involve looking differently at what has been in front of you for a very long time.
(Photo by Robert Els for Quechua Benefit)

It matters what you focus on. It might involve looking differently at what has been in front of you for a very long time. It might mean focusing on what might have been ignored until now. Just as focusing on the spaces between the raindrops gave a clear view of the road ahead, perhaps focusing on something you might have missed up until now might free you to recognize the Divine, the clear path, and the way forward. It certainly may not be helpful to allow the obstacles (raindrops) that obscure the view to be the focus of your attention.

Having a purpose, goals, or mission is life changing. Having the interest and drive to start, pursue, and maintain the energy to accomplish something pleasurable and important can

24

become the purpose of life itself for some people. Even if a purpose is relatively short lived or limited, such as finishing college, finding a new house, driving in the rain with no windshield wipers, or collecting sea glass from a shipwreck, it can enrich your every moment while you are focused on it.

I suggest you open yourself to having a purpose to seek the Divine in your everyday life. You can look for and recognize the Divine in both old and new places. Think about it. Draw pictures of it. Sing about it. Pray for it. Talk about it. Write about it. This concept may help you on your path, *Your life is constantly filled with the presence of the Divine.* Fortunately, we have some help in finding God.

God speaks in a unique language. Learn to recognize this language of God. It can be soft and gentle or harsh and loud, full of symbols and meaning, and it speaks to you all the time. It may come to you in chance meetings, opportunities, words, images, impactful events, stories, recurring things, dreams, joyous favorite pleasures, and any number of mysterious coincidences.

Perhaps it was the language of God that the encounters on the beach opened up just as I was about to begin writing this book. Perhaps it was in the language of God to have the experience of looking past the raindrops to see clearly. Could that have stuck with me as a peak experience because there was a lesson to learn? Isn't it interesting that both the events I chose to share in this beginning chapter have to do with glass? Could the Divine want me to share with you so you may *see clearly?*

In the language of God, symbols have meaning. Listen for the language of God and understand it in ways that will be so personal and pure that there is no doubt that the Light is

25

abundantly present. This book will help you look at these things in new and meaningful ways.

Deep within us is a reservoir, hidden from the world and sometimes even hidden from ourselves. It is filled from the Source that fills all our reservoirs, and it never runs dry. It is a deep well that offers to quench our thirst if we allow ourselves to drink. We can ignore it if we wish, or we can sip from it selectively. If we ask, it cools and comforts us. If we give it permission, it shows us who we are, where we come from, and where we are going. Though it speaks in a language almost foreign to us, it invites our understanding. (written by Barry Morley)

Maybe we don't know how to listen to the language of God. Perhaps we once knew and then forgot. Then, there's the problem of language. Can you understand a foreign language? Perhaps the concept *God speaks to us in a mysterious language that we can learn* can help us realize meaning. We learn nonverbal sound messages—a car horn, ambulance siren, ice cream truck bell. Perhaps we don't know what to listen for. A bird expert can pick out the song of just one bird, where the untrained ear might not be able to distinguish that sound from the many singing birds.

Perhaps we are afraid to listen to God. Are you afraid God might ask you to do something you don't want to do? God might ask big, dangerous things. Can you realize God loves you so much that you wouldn't be asked to do something you don't want to? Or are you afraid you will listen and there will be nothing there?

What would it mean for you to look for the Divine as never before, to change your idea of God? What if you could no longer just check off attending a required religious service, or

26

say a standard prayer as your completed God connection? What if there was so much more connection available? Consider what it would be like to take some time to look through the chaos of your life and become aware of the unique relationship you have with the Presence that is right in front of you. For people who have tried this, some didn't find anything because they forgot to focus. Once they remembered to focus, they had results. If we can turn our awareness on, just by remembering to, we might find a simple (though not easy) way to be more purposeful. Being mindful of your purpose and keeping focused on your search may need some assistance to maintain your new pursuit. Try putting a dot of ink somewhere on the palm of your hand, choose a word or sound to repeat in your head, or imagine a loving companion by your side to guide you. You can choose any gentle reminder that may help.

In my counseling practice, my clients sometimes express their desire for a greater bond with the God of their understanding. They reflect on their beliefs about their spiritual paths. They feel the experience of just being alive at this time and in this place and make a connection with others who are also in the here and now. Some believe that their spiritual path connects with all the other paths, like a weaving that makes a beautiful tapestry. Some ask the question, "Why even pray?" They prefer the idea of a constant connection with Spirit rather than the on-and-off of prayer. Others view God as Creator and Parent, which makes the relationship more personal and ongoing. There are clients who, when looking for God in new ways, experience an increase in disturbing and negative experiences. They ask themselves how becoming more aware of Presence can fuel this unexpected result.

It might be harder to find that loving, caring Presence when times are tough, when times are bad, and you are so down that

27

sometimes the only thing that seems real is the emptiness and darkness. This may happen any time.

Imagine if you have been working, perhaps for a while, with your eye on a job with promotion potential, prestige, and position working closely with the big boss. I know someone for whom this was a dream and a goal. That dream was dashed when someone else was given the plum job. Such disappointment and loss, such self-doubt and discouragement followed.

Maybe we don't know how to listen to the language of God, or perhaps we once knew and then forgot.
(Photo by Robert Els for Quechua Benefit)

Where was the Divine in those horrible feelings?

After a short time, the new person who got the job had to take a two-month leave, and guess who was asked to be the substitute? Yes, it was the disappointed employee who didn't get the job initially. The two-month period began and almost immediately there were clashes of personality, pressure to perform ethical breaches, and long lonely hours redoing excellent work to meet impossible standards. By the end of the two months, the disappointed employee was so grateful that the job was not permanent, and it wouldn't become the horrible reality it surely would have been. And yet, I imagine during that most discouraging time, it was hard to feel that loving Divine closeness.

28

Where was God in the handful of pills swallowed in private to end one's painful life? Was it in those who discovered the almost-dead friend? In the ambulance with the EMTs? With the doctor who wouldn't take no for an answer after several failed attempts to shove the life-saving tube down a closed throat? With the mother who was the first face seen after days waiting for a coma to lift? Where was God in the decision to never cause others so much anguish or take one's own precious life for granted? Fred Rogers of *Mister Rogers' Neighborhood* fame shared his mother's wisdom: In difficult times, always look for the helpers. There are helpers, and that's where the Divine touches our lives—even when the suffering of the moment keeps us from realizing it.

It is unlikely you will have the same experiences that have been shared here. How could you when your relationship with God is unique to you? I wonder what will be opened up for you if you give yourself some time to increase your awareness.

You might become convinced that *your life is constantly filled with the presence of the Divine.* In the next chapter, we will explore looking forward to ways in which we become open to looking for something. As you reflect on this chapter, continue to ponder. How comfortable are you in the undefined realm of accepting that God is a mystery? Have you had a Divine feeling or encounter that you considered a direct connection from or with God? When do you feel God's presence? When do you feel God's absence? How does God communicate with you?

Concepts

Looking for Something

God is a mystery.

The Divine will appear to you in ways that only you recognize.

Your life is constantly filled with the presence of the Divine.

God speaks to us in a mysterious language that we can learn.

Chapter 2
Favorite Things

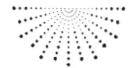

Remember that song from *The Sound of Music* about all of Maria's favorite things? She sang of her love for raindrops on roses, and whiskers on kittens ... and on and on. It was a long list. The lyrics tell us that dog bites, bee stings, and sad feelings aren't so bad when she simply remembers her favorite things. Sometimes, as the song indicates, thinking of favorite things can turn around the pain of negative experiences. Favorite things can make you feel happy. Let's look at an underlying concept supporting favorite things and build on a powerful and positive way of thinking, *God wants all good for you.*

It's an intriguing part of a spiritual quest to probe the nature of the Divine, which can be a challenge, given we have already said the *Divine is a mystery!* I trust that *God wants all good for me.* This concept prompts some very interesting ideas. I accept that God does not cause harm or good. Many people believe the Great Spirit to be a puppeteer, holding the strings that direct all the events in our lives. That would make God responsible for wars, not curing the sick, and allowing painful things in your life to happen. That line of thinking then leads

31

God wants all good for you.
(Photo by Katie Safley for Quechua Benefit)

us to ask, "Why would God do that?" with the answer most closely aligning to the view that humans sin, and God punishes.

Wanting good for another is not the same as being able to cause good (or evil). If my beloved friend is suffering a personal tragedy, I want good for them, but I am unable to undo the tragedy, just as I was not able to prevent it. There is much written about the reason bad things happen. I accept the randomness of all life, the law of natural consequences, and the chaos that results in both bad and good things happening. One way that good becomes manifest is in God providing us with the joy of *favorites*.

Let's first recollect a euphoric feeling you might have had as a child. Regardless of your actual life experience, we all can imagine this vision. Consider the joy of that feeling if you are

32

five and it is your birthday, and all the presents are for you, and all your friends are coming for your party. Yep. It's that feeling. Not every day is like that imaginary fifth birthday party. Yet you have the option to enjoy your favorite things any day. So how do you notice your favorites? Let's look at a way of capturing the experiences and feelings that give us the sense of connecting with the mystery of God through recognizing our favorite things.

For me, it actually can be as simple as whiskers on kittens. I have a crazy dog, and my boyfriend has a crazy dog. The dogs love each other and play like puppies. It gives me the happiest feeling of carefree, loving, joyful abandon to watch them. They make me laugh. I've seen them do it hundreds of times, and it fills me with delight every time. (I think that is God giving me a treat and letting me know that sometimes the Spirit which passes through all things does it just for fun.) For someone else it is the look, smell, and sound of the fall leaves. It can be looking out your back window and seeing the deer that come up to the window and peer in at you. How delightful!

I like the shape of a heart, and much of my jewelry is heart-shaped, as is the wreath on my door and an ornament in my yard, and on and on. It fills me with such a good feeling to see that shape.

Remember when Forrest Gump said life was like a box of chocolates? Favorite things are like a sampler of chocolates. Favorite colors, numbers, phrases, songs, poems, Bible verses, stories, movies, all your favorites are like the Divine handing out those chocolates—just so you know that Presence is always there for you. Every time you encounter a favorite, think of it as a gift from God.

33

Sometimes these favorites appear in the little day-to-day things, but other times, these favorite gifts come in great big ways in life. They can come in peak experiences, life-changing directions, or surprising turns of events. Let's look at some of the favorite things that are universal, and that also connect in such significant ways with *all good* things that God gives us as favorites. These favorites include the love of learning and growing, being in our bodies, being an artistic creator, and connecting with nature.

Have you ever had the feeling that you are connecting perfectly with learning and growing? I have, which forms the next concept, which tells us that *God wants us to learn and grow.* Our favorite things can lead us to the joy of that experience. There are so many ways to experience that feeling, and sometimes it actually happens in school. It didn't feel like any connections happened for me in all of high school, or when I flunked out my freshman year in college, or when I went back and had to take all those college "101" requirements. There were still no felt connections when I decided on a major only based on what I thought would be the one I was least likely to fail.

Even though schooling had long been one of my least favorite things, it surprisingly transformed into an exceptional favorite thing. The day I took a survey course in 17th Century British poetry, I began to learn and grow, after which I took every 17th Century course I could. The 17th Century in England was the time of the great leap into metaphysical thinking—a spiritual and holistic way of looking at oneself and the world. These ideas touched me at an emotional, spiritual, and intellectual level that was on fire with excitement, natural motivation, joy, interest, and unabashed enthusiasm.

34

That great connection happened again when I was in counseling school and studied Alfred Adler, a colleague of Freud, who believed people had the natural potential for health and greatness within them and that it was the counselor's job to provide the encouragement for that to blossom. I connected with this philosophy at such a centered place within me that it was in sync with my every heartbeat. I wrote a paper on Adlerian philosophy, and I got the one and only A+ in my life. That's connection!

I have also experienced times of massive disconnect. My early life took a left turn into, of all things, dentistry. I became a dental assistant after flunking out of college. I even went on to teach it once I had my bachelor's degree, but for me, the work was dry, boring, dull, and lifeless. It offered no potential for new and creative job experiences. Into that grayness, God presented a spark. Remember, *God wants us to learn and grow.*

By chance, one day at a dental conference in Boston, I signed up for a course on Whole Brain Learning. I probably took it because it was more interesting to me than the more

dreadful dental offerings. To my amazement, the course opened my understanding about how to enlighten learning. It showed how to turn learning into fun by creating games, using art, giving control to the

God wants us to learn and grow.
(Photo by Robert Els for Quechua Benefit)

35

student, and honoring the learning process as a dynamic, delightful gift. From my perspective, it put the Spirit front and center.

I found my whole being turned on in that class, and I took that learning back to my dull classroom and redesigned all my courses to be entertaining and enjoyable. I loved doing the redesign, teaching became a passion, and the lively, engaging way my students reacted filled my heart with joy.

As I learned more about this process and created more and more ways to implement fun and creativity into my classes, my mastery of whole brain learning qualified me to enter my next phase of growth, once I left the university and dentistry. I joined a Fortune 500 company, Marriott Corporation, to design leadership and management development programs. It shouldn't surprise you that these programs were filled with games, fun, and dynamic ways for new managers to learn about themselves and others and to grow.

In retrospect, I appreciate that even though I had gotten off track in the dental field, I was Divinely led to a new path about to give me great joy, and I had support to encounter the next steps on my journey unearthing yet another favorite. This passage from bored dental assistant to lively management trainer reminds me that even when we may get off track and disengage from the God-part of us for a while, something can open up to allow us to discover the Divine that is abundant, ever present, and within.

Had I paid more attention to my motivation to enter the dental field, I would have known I was heading in a not-favorite direction. Remember, I was in high school, finding school insufferable. My neighbor was a 20-year-old recent graduate from dental hygiene school. She was cool. She had

36

her own car. And the greatest thing of all was she wore a uniform. I didn't have a clue as to what to pursue in college, and a two-year degree that would lead to coolness seemed as good as anything, so I set my direction for dental hygiene. The curriculum was heavy in the sciences (one of my two weaknesses, math being the other). Quickly, I was flunking out and felt really miserable. I then took a technical course in dental assisting at the same college, which I just barely tolerated. I was elected class president, and I did a miserable job at that.

What I have come to know about *God wanting us to learn and grow* and how that relates to favorite things is that the clue to the best path forward is to search for the joy in the choice to lead you to a favorite thing. As soon as you possibly can, embrace that you deserve the goodness that is abundant.

God seems to like throwing an unexpected favorite thing right at us from time to time. I grew up in the city, then as an adult I lived in the suburbs, and I liked both.

"I've always wanted land," my former husband said one day when I was into middle age.

Why not? I thought.

We moved to the country. Then we decided to get an alpaca. I know, that seems to be a giant leap, but there was Divine direction there, too, without question.

Before getting married, I had adopted both my children from Peru. When thinking about how fun it would be to have farm animals, I remembered seeing alpacas in Peru. After a click on Google and a few visits to alpaca farms, we got an alpaca. Eventually, we had 42. We also had farm help to manage, fences to build, sick animals to care for, animals to

37

breed and birth, and buyers, marketing, and advertising to coordinate. And soon we were taking home blue ribbons and championships from the show circuit. Before long, I went from not knowing anything about an alpaca to running a full agricultural business—and loving it. Who knew that would become a favorite thing?

Have you had something just thrown at you, something you never really asked for, but one thing led to another and before you knew it, there you were? That, my friend, was Divine presence, the hand of God, and Spiritual connection far beyond the sample of everyday things. You got a beautiful favorite thing, wrapped up with a bow, and given as a gift, and it wasn't even your fifth birthday! Having the alpacas to care for was surely a favorite thing and a Divine gift for me.

Have you ever had the feeling that your physical body was in perfect harmony with movement? Our bodies are certainly a favorite thing from the Divine. Certainly, the next concept speaks clearly that *the Divine wants us to enjoy our bodies*. I am so low on the athletic scale that my constant fear in high school was that I would be the last one picked for the team in gym class. So, when I picked up tennis in my late twenties, it was remarkable in itself that I looked into something that involved sneakers and aerobic breathing.

I liked it. I even liked it a lot, and I didn't stink at it. I met fun people and looked forward to going into league playing. I took lessons, paid for equipment, and learned a game I had never played. That happened again when I had to get in shape for back surgery, and out of desperation I started going to a water aerobics class. Again, this was something I had never done. I wasn't horrible at it, and I liked it. It made me feel healthy and alive.

What have you found that fits your body just right and allowed you to experience the harmony of movement in your body? Was it dance? Walking? Kickboxing? Strength training?

The Biblical story of creation is so fundamental to our understanding of the Spirit Which Passes Through All Things and its relationship with each of us that it isn't surprising that we, too, yearn to create. We have a universal desire to connect to that which we call art. We deem as a favorite thing our drive to express beauty, emotion, and meaning through artistic creations. We experience the creative arts opening the connection between our earthly, bodily, survival-mode existence and the dimension sometimes called heaven. It doesn't take much searching to experience the next concept describing a favorite thing, *The creative arts invite us to touch the face of the Divine.* Whether painting, music, dance, or the many creative activities in which we may engage, the creative arts raise us to understand our partnership with the Creator. That feeling is transformative. To be the creator or performer is to experience an almost out-of-body sensation that has no equal.

The arts have so much power that you don't even have to be the creator. Listening to great music, viewing beautiful art or dance, or just being close to them can give you that euphoric feeling. I think of the performances I have attended and had that rush, the high, the tingling from the inside out as the witness of a transcendent experience.

I have also had that privilege once in my life to experience the transcendence as an actual performer. The inaugural performance at Wolf Trap Center for Performing Arts outside of Washington, D.C., in the early 1970s, featured pianist Van Cliburn, with Julius Rudel conducting the New York City

39

Opera with Norman Treigle. There were performances by the National Symphony Orchestra and the Choral Arts Society of Washington. I sang with the Choral Arts Society. I stood on the first riser, stage left, at the end. The closing performance was a massive choral work with Van Cliburn as pianist and the National Symphony Orchestra creating music that was intense, magnificent, and sublimely exquisite. For me to perform the choral part, my tiny part among the hundreds of musicians and the finest of performers at the opening night of a unique yet-to-be-famous venue, created an out-of-body sensation beyond anything I could have imagined. I was there and not there. I was one with everyone, yet all alone. In every fiber of my being, I was alive, connected, and transformed.

Even though that was a one-time experience, those same feelings come over me when seeing the pain and tenderness in Michelangelo's sculpture the *Pietà* in St. Peter's Basilica in Rome and when experiencing the passion in Camille Claudel's sculpture *The Kiss* that overshadows Rodin's by far, or listening to Bach's *Magnificat*, reading great literature, or watching the Alvin Ailey dancers.

What ignites your inner passion? Is it a simple and lovely joy that feels just right? Is it that overwhelming transformation into another world? Wouldn't you like to capture that and bottle it so you could take it out anytime you want? Start listening to beautiful music, reading great works, seeing fabulous art, and watching sublime dance. The Divine is within you, and it awakens within you when you engage in the arts.

We often refer to the Divine as the Creator. The Bible tells us God created the heavens and the Earth. Our relationship with nature—the earth we walk on, plants and animals, our air and atmosphere—is a favorite thing. Being in nature is another

40

experience that brings Spirit close for many people. There are so many favorites in nature. Who doesn't love the beach, the mountains, unspoiled wilderness, and connecting with plants and animals? It isn't surprising that the beauty of flowers touches many with the miracle of growth and the magnificence of form and color. This love of nature leads us to the concept *Connecting with nature unites us with the Divine.*

I heard about a very brave person who, after a tragic loss, pursued her healing through gardening. The healing led her to teach gardening to others. I know someone who took a course in perennial design with her. Perennials come up every year, after planting them only once. The course became a significant favorite experience, and the results were very special. The student met nice people—a prediction her mother made—she learned what it meant to have roots and to know what hope is. If you look up the properties of roots and of perennials, it becomes apparent that this is a weighty symbol with deeper meaning than just the literal garden definitions.

Consider when you have had a loss, how fragile your roots have felt. Permanence, the key characteristic of perennials, seems sometimes all but lost when experiencing tragedy. The association with perennials became a favorite thing for both teacher and student.

The healing that started with the teacher was passed to the student. The student then took the design to a new home, planted a new perennial garden, continuing the healing. When we look at what makes perennials extraordinary, consider their qualities. From a small seed, they grow with beauty, rest in winter, and return not just next spring, but every spring. There isn't any question about them being a loving favorite that shows the continuance of the Divine's gifts to us.

41

Our relationship with nature—the earth we walk on, plants and animals, our air and atmosphere—is a favorite thing.
(Photo by Alejandro Tejeda for Quechua Benefit)

How many times have you been in the dark place of ashes, the place that seems so empty? It is in that place that you might experience the next concept, *The Spirit will lead you, guide you, push you, and open the way for you.* The significance of this concept is powerful. We don't always know what will become a favorite, or what is all good for us. Sometimes we have to be shown the way. Sometimes we have to be pushed toward discovering our favorite thing.

The consulting practice that I had before becoming a parent demanded travel. Once my first daughter was born, I had to find work without travel. I was a single parent, having

42

adopted my daughter (and later her sister) from Peru, and my lifestyle and job had to accommodate my family.

A client, a local bank, hired me as a consultant, then offered me a full-time job. It was just what I wanted and needed at the time. I started in a position where I was using my creativity to design management development training programs and doing organizational development interventions. I was grateful for the job, even though in the four years I had been there, it was becoming a bit bland. Then it went from bland, to bad, to worse when the company downsized, and my department reorganized.

After the reorganization, I was asked to manage the newly formed automation department—the precursor to an IT office. That change took me from job duties that were becoming lifeless to job responsibilities I was in no way able to tolerate.

The organization's downsizing process surprisingly gave me a little boost when I was asked to assist the newly-let-go (now former employees) gain some help and dignity. I designed and facilitated a weeklong workshop for them on how to recover from losing their jobs. The people who came to that workshop were devastated. Being with them at this really difficult time was an honor and privilege I had never experienced before. Their pain and hope touched me. The caring came naturally to me, and my compassion for them lasted long after the week. I was transformed.

Returning to automation technology became agony for me. I was sensing I was at the end of my career and my job. What could I do when I had little children—aged two and four years old—who depended on me entirely to bring home the one and only full-time paycheck?

43

A friend of mine mentioned a local program in pastoral counseling that was only a few years old. Might that be of interest to me? I made a call to the program and asked them to mail a brochure. The day it came is still a powerful memory for me. The pretty blue and white cover and soft feel was just the invitation to open it. As I read the course offerings, I felt that connected feeling again. There was another Presence with me. I was not alone. As I absorbed the descriptions of the student body, faculty, courses, and goals, I felt a centering within me that was like that sweet spot when the tennis ball and the racquet connect perfectly. It was a sacred experience.

Unquestionably, this was the right step on my path. But how? I had no extra money, I couldn't go to school while I was working my dreadful job, but I wouldn't have any money if I gave up my job.

I talked to God and made a deal. Knowing there was no way this would work if I used good judgment or common sense, for the first time in my life I gave up control over my own decisions. Here was the bargain, if God opened the door, I would walk through. I would take the step on the path that was in front of me. If God presented a brick wall, I promised I would not bash my head in, not bloody myself, not cry, ask why, or get mad. I would just quietly turn away from the wall and go another way.

I kept my word, and God kept opening doors that appeared to be miracles one after another. Money came from the most unusual places, sometimes when there were only minutes to go before plunging into impossibility. Just enough local consulting work came my way. Scholarships materialized out of thin air. I gave up my bedroom for two years and slept on the sofa so I could rent out my bedroom in exchange for

44

free evening babysitting that allowed me to attend classes at night when I could. Another seemingly marvel was that the perfect person showed up to do the bedroom rental and babysitting. I even found a telephone buddy who was going to a different school. We talked every night at midnight for a study break amid regular study hours between 10 PM and 2 AM.

It was so clear that Spirit wanted me to learn and grow and was there every step of the way. I started the graduate program when my girls were two and four years old. I graduated three years later, went on for another year of advanced study, while taking low-paying part-time jobs two at a time. One day, I was offered the full-time job of a lifetime, complete with a paycheck, benefits, and retirement to see me through. I have loved the field of pastoral counseling and have practiced it ever since.

When have you taken that leap of faith when common sense said "No"? When have you let the Divine take over in times of uncertainty or despair? When have you let a favorite thing guide you to the sweet spot you were meant to experience? What would it take to be a sign? How many favorite things would it take for you to pay attention and go forward?

I know someone for whom butterflies are symbols of her mother, who passed when my friend was only a teenager. The mother had a tattoo of a butterfly, something, I was told, that was not in keeping with her usual style, however, butterflies had become one of her favorite things. When I saw my friend recently, she was feeling especially close to the memories of her mother. We talked about her mother for a long time. She said one thing she recently experienced was a bit unusual. She had been seeing butterflies everywhere. She saw them when

45

she was walking, driving, working, and playing, when she was alone and when she was with others—all the time!

What if there were something that was very special for you? What if it had meaning and evoked feelings of love and caring for you? What if you started seeing it, or hints of it, frequently and in the most unusual places? Your favorite things will find you, just as God's love surrounds you.

Think of the people in your life who are most special. How do you show them how special you think they are? You may give them presents, take them to special places, search for experiences and items that you know will give them joy, prepare surprises for them, honor their current favorites by creating opportunities to give them. You might even create ways for them to add new favorites to their lives. The Divine does that, too. Spirit loves you so very much and wants you to know that.

How many times in families with many children have the siblings vied for status as "the favorite"? We don't have to do that with God. Each of us is a favorite. God gives us these special moments and experiences as a way, each time, to tell us we are loved. Our joy is God's joy. God

Each of us is a favorite.
(Photo by Robert Els for Quechua Benefit)

delights when we have these feelings that lift our hearts and souls to remind us of the essence of our own divine nature.

As you reflect on this chapter, continue to ponder. What are your favorite things? Have you considered they may be a gift from the Divine? If you accept that God wants all good for you, how does that help you recognize your favorites? When you learn something new and wonderful, how does that connect you with Spirit? Are you a body with a spirit or a spirit with a body? How do you enjoy your body? How do the creative arts transform you? What parts of nature are your favorite? Have you ever been dragged, kicking and screaming, into something wonderful?

Concepts

Favorite Things

God wants all good for you.

God wants us to learn and grow.

The Divine wants us to enjoy our bodies.

The creative arts invite us to touch the face of the Divine.

Connecting with nature unites us with the Divine.

The Spirit will lead you, guide you, push you, and open the way for you.

47

Chapter 3
Divine Persistence

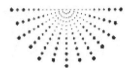

Persistence is about being devoted and tireless. The Divine is a champion of repeated lessons, second chances, and tenacious support. The stunning creation of our precious Earth gives us immeasurable examples of cycles and patterns that repeat. How unreal our lives might have been with a God who expected us to learn important life lessons with only one chance, or who gave us the beauty of nature for only a moment. You don't even want to imagine a harsh Creator telling you the following:

> You have one—only one—chance to do the most important thing ever. If you fail, you will never get the opportunity again to do this most important thing. Everything depends on your doing it perfectly without knowledge, experience, or practice. Are you ready?

> I'll give you a minute before you start, but only one minute. The clock is ticking, and as you have read this, you have used up part of your time. Remember, this is the most important

thing ever, and the only acceptable level is perfection. Ready, set, GO!

Oh dear, you didn't make it. Your chance is now over. So sorry!

Or perhaps the following from that harsh Creator:

> I want to show you a stunning sunrise. You will be blown away with its beauty and splendor. You will be transformed and amazed. This, however, will be your one and only chance to see it, and it will be gone forever. The sky will be blank for ever after. I sure hope you will enjoy this once-in-a-lifetime sunrise.

Can you imagine what our lives would be like if this were the way God set up creation? Instead, we get many repeated chances to learn, grow, and understand. We can fall down, fail, get up, and try again. If it's a lesson we need to learn about life, and we don't get it right at first, circumstances certainly come around again and again, giving us many opportunities. Redundancy is God's way of saying, "Wake up. Recognize that I am speaking to you. Listen to me. I love you so much. I will be persistent and will not give up on you. I will give you many lessons in your life, abundant chances to achieve happiness, and I will sustain you and hold you close—especially in your neediest times."

Persistence is about being devoted and tireless.
(Photo by Robert Els for Quechua Benefit)

49

The Divine surrounds us with abundant opportunities that repeat. I started to think of all the repeating things we take for granted. For example, when one second passes, we get another one in the next second. Consider how the following repeat in our lives: seconds, minutes, hours, days, weeks, months, years, seasons, sunrises, sunsets, the need to eat and drink, women's cycles, blinking, going to work, encounters with friends, merry-go-rounds, refrains in poems and songs, perennial flowers, tides, phases of the moon, watching favorite movies over and over, and saying "I love you." A good life is filled with all the second chances we have had. All these patterns of repetition are some of the ways the Divine is persistent about supporting our spiritual growth, which is how we can embrace the next concept, *Repeated lessons are a gift from God.*

Like most of you, I had to take math in school. You already know that math is not a strength of mine. Even as I listened to the teacher, I got nothing. I gave up asking questions because I didn't understand enough to formulate a question. My experience was devasting. It had a powerful effect on me, making me feel as though I had no ability to understand math. I knew it was the lack in me, not the teacher. I remember feeling as though a breeze, meant to catch a sail and give it momentum and direction, went through my brain as if that sail were a screen door. Nothing happened, although the teacher and I kept trying. Luckily, I was given the opportunity to have a tutor. I could listen as the tutor repeated each lesson, explaining each concept again, and offered me the chance to practice math problems over and over.

I grew to understand math. I knew that no matter what the math subject, or who the teacher, I couldn't understand anything the first time through. I had a math tutor for every math class I took from middle school through two master's

50

degrees. My brain just cannot learn math with only a one-time lesson. With repetition, I gained knowledge, understanding, and the ability to think in a new language. Perhaps recognizing the Divine in our lives is similar to learning a different language, as we need reminding of the Presence over and over, and over again.

A belief that is based on repeating something until we understand it is called karma (also spelled kharma). In Hinduism and Buddhism, simply put, all of a person's actions and conduct during successive incarnations cause or at least influence her or his destiny. Karma can act in multiple feedback loops (times and experiences that repeat if the issues behind them are not resolved), with the present moment being shaped both by past and by present actions while also influencing the future.

With karma there is also free will, although its range is somewhat dictated by the past. The nature of this freedom is symbolized in an image used by the early Buddhists: flowing water. Sometimes the flow from the past is so strong that little can be done except to stand fast against the stream, but other times the flow is gentle enough to be diverted in almost any direction.

Of course, for karma to exist, there has to be repetition of existence. Simply said, if you don't achieve a satisfactory level of enlightenment in one lifetime, your soul comes back after a completed lifetime. You then may have another opportunity to learn in a future lifetime with a different body.

I am on the fence about reincarnation, but it isn't a far-out theory to me. I am amazed by the big miracle and leap of faith it takes to grasp one-time incarnation, which is pretty much universally accepted. Combining the physical formation of the

51

body and the indwelling addition of the soul can take a huge leap of faith to accept. Reincarnation, then, is just the repetition of that sacred miracle. Some Christians accept the anticipated second coming—the reincarnation of Jesus.

Another miracle that most people freely accept is that new humans and animals have the ability to keep the species regenerating as they continue to have babies. (Which is another form of repetition!) That's incredible just in itself.

We can't see, hear, or touch the soul, but we can feel it. Perhaps it is the spark of the Divine that connects us with every living or existing form on Earth. Many traditional Christians believe that the soul of Jesus visited Earth after his death. His soul appears to Mary Magdalene and the "other Mary" at the tomb, the disciples on a mountain in Galilee (or Jerusalem), to Cleopas and an unnamed disciple on the road to Emmaus, and to Peter and other disciples together.

The Bible makes numerous references to the soul. The soul is defined as the breath of God and part of God. Genesis 2:7 says, "Then the Lord God formed the man of dust from the ground and breathed into his nostrils the breath of life, and the man became a living creature." Ecclesiastes 12:7 says, "And the dust returns to the earth as it was, and the spirit returns to God who gave it."

However, you may interpret this Biblical information, the significant belief to hold on to is the existence of the soul and the formation of the body. Once you have accepted your own version of how that is meaningful to you, reincarnation is only about that repeating. I find it interesting how so many people accept the body and soul phenomenon (incarnation) but reject the doing-it-again (reincarnation) portion.

52

Of course, it is not necessary for you to believe in reincarnation at all. Plenty of opportunities exist to experience karma right in this lifetime. The repetition of past, present, and future floats around you constantly. Although life is constantly changing, it is also endlessly repeating. In the karmic mindset, there is also the famous quotation, often credited to philosopher George Santayana, "Those who cannot remember the past are condemned to repeat it." That quote is often reworded to say, "Those who do not learn from history are doomed to repeat it."

Redundancy is God's way of saying, "I love you so much, I will be persistent and will not give up on you."
(Photo by Robert Els for Quechua Benefit)

In addition to the persistence through repetitions that the Divine presents to us, we also create repetitions in our own lives on purpose because we love them. They become some of our favorite things, and we call them traditions. We begin with an idea, then we do something to bring the idea to life that is special to us. Then we repeat it.

Have you ever built a tradition? Did you create it on purpose, or did you just start repeating something and before

53

you realized it you and others started anticipating it and then worked to re-create it. Perhaps you would refine it, adjust it, or improve it, but the one thing that made it a tradition was that it was repeated.

The reason a tradition becomes special is it gives you the feeling of resonance. This is similar to the feeling we have when we have that special feeling of being close to the Divine. Resonance is vibrant, deep, full, and powerful, with special meaning and importance. The feeling of resonance that comes with a treasured tradition expands our sense that this special, persistent, and repeated tradition is a spiritual gift and leads to our next concept, *Repetition with Divine resonance becomes tradition.*

A well-known movie made in 1993 involves the quintessential lesson in repeated experiences and second chances. Groundhog Day stars Bill Murray as Phil Connors, a TV weatherman who, during an assignment covering the annual Groundhog Day event, is caught in a time loop, repeatedly living the same day. Phil wakes up every day to the same song on the radio. He spends the first few days in an unbelieving stupor until he finally realizes he is really repeating the same day. Once he accepts that he is in this continuum, he goes on to pursue as much mischief as he can get away with. In time, he starts to use his predicament for good. He learns skills such as playing the piano, speaking French, and studying history. It is only when he eventually comes to terms with the true values of loving and accepting himself and others that he can move on.

I am intrigued by this movie because it speaks to so many things in life that we have to learn the hard way, by making mistakes or poor choices and then living with the

54

consequences over and over until we finally take the high road in our own lives and act differently, hoping for positive outcomes. Many of the repeated lessons and second chances we are given make known the following concept, *Persistence is one of the many ways the Divine reveals itself.*

Another story is told in the movie *About Time,* made in 2013. Tim (played by Domhnall Gleeson) discovers, at age 21, that he can travel in time and change what will happen and what has happened in his own life. His decision to make his world a better place by getting a girlfriend turns out not to be as easy as he thought. Whenever Tim makes a blunder, he is able to go back to the beginning of the blunder and re-do his thinking and actions, thereby changing the cause and effect. After many experiences, he learns that if he does the right thing in the first place, he doesn't have to repeat the event. When he practices patience, kindness, gratitude, compassion, and empathy, he moves forward in real time without remorse or regret.

How are you with recognizing and dealing with the patterns in your life? What events or trials do you find repeating in your life? If you look at the things you would like to redo and events you would like to relive, what are the lessons you need to learn and wish for?

I look at the things I would do differently and see very powerful lessons. I wish I hadn't smoked cigarettes at age 16. The lesson was to respect my body and my health. My parents both smoked and forbade me to smoke, which made it a very attractive rebellion. I could smoke in designated places on my high school grounds, with a very accepting group of fellow smokers who welcomed me. What could be better than rebellion, acceptance, and appearing more grown up?

55

One day, about 20 years later, I was coming back from the hospital where my mother had just undergone a heart angioplasty, a few years after my father had part of a lung removed due to cancer. I made a different decision than the one that seemed attractive at age 16. I quit smoking for life.

It may not have been as close to a Hollywood experience as Tim in About Time, but I was finally able to end those disappointing days and have my redo. An unhealthy, expensive, smelly, and socially distancing activity vanished instantly.

Another poor decision was my selection of a college. I wish I had chosen to go to an outstanding university when I received my letter of acceptance. At 17 years old, I doubted myself, and I didn't have the confidence that I could meet the high standards of an excellent program. Instead of going to that established, reputable school in my major, I chose a small, fledgling college with no academic record and entered a program in its maiden year. With inexperienced faculty and staff who didn't help when I found myself unmotivated and struggling academically, I flunked out my freshman year. Looking back, my lesson was living with the negative consequences of thinking less of myself, and eventually learning to acknowledge my worth and worthiness years later when faced with a similar choice.

Without degree or direction, I took a job in an office that went nowhere with no opportunity for growth. I fell in love with a young man who had just graduated from law school. I was hoping for a future together, when he told me he couldn't take me home to his professional, educated parents because I hadn't finished college. It took me just one day to make a vow that I would never be limited in life from the lack of a college

56

degree. I would go back at night for as long as it took and pay for it myself so my parents would never be burdened. It just took one day to make that vow, and eventually I had an associate's degree, bachelor's degree, and two master's degrees. The redo began that one day when I made that vow.

I wish I had waited for a deeply committed and spiritually connected marriage partner. I could have had faith in my worth and my ability to love myself. Instead, I chose marriage for reasons that came from my place of lack and need. After a very painful realization that all the hope, adjusting, coping, and time would not make anything better in a long toxic marriage relationship, one day the words *I don't want to be married to you anymore* came spilling out of my mouth. And with that one decision, I started building a safe, happy, and loving future.

We get our do-overs. We get to heal our regrets. We get this because God gives us so many second chances, so many new days, so many repeated opportunities to get better. Our past, our present moments, and our futures are continuous.

If you don't pay attention to the Divine in your everyday life one way, God might just evoke Divine persistence to make you take notice. We therefore begin understanding the concept *God will use all available means to get our attention.* For me, my mother and father's poor health got my attention to decide to quit smoking, a brief failed relationship with a boyfriend got my attention to return to school, and suffering in an emotionally harmful marriage led to inner peace. God never gives up on you, not ever. Even at your lowest point, the Divine is present. A powerful, ever-present way the Spirit grabs our attention is through the gift of repetition. We keep getting a new day regardless of how we use it or waste it. A person who

57

lives until 80 years old has more than 29,000 days to make choices to start and end a day differently than the day before. When we recognize God's love and presence, we notice ample reminders all around. God gives

We get our do-overs. We heal our regrets.
(Photo by Robert Els for Quechua Benefit)

us a sense of time by the repeated gifts of nature over which we have no control. The sunrise, seasons, and tides continue without our hand. Consider the idea that something may not necessarily happen in your desired time or in your desired way, but with the timing and purpose of the Divine.

What does God's tenacious support mean when we focus on recognizing the Divine in our everyday lives? It means we are so loved by a God who will do everything possible to help us be our very best. Our Light is indwelling to nourish us, and it shines outward to the world. It also means the Spirit sustains us during our failures and difficult times by being an encouraging and loving presence, helping us to become better and happier no matter how long it takes. The concept that speaks to the Divine's tenacity is *God's persistence is present even when we are unaware.*

Don't you love the story of "Footprints"? In it, the speaker paints a poignant picture of a dream. While walking on a beach, scenes of their* life appear in a dark sky as a flash, and for each scene there are two sets of footprints in the sand—one belonging to the dreamer and one to God. When all the

58

scenes of their life pass, they look back at the footprints in the sand and notice that at the saddest and most difficult times of their life there was only one set of footprints.

The speaker, troubled and distraught, asks the Divine why, when they had devoted their life to faith in God, would they be abandoned? Why, when most needed, would God leave their life path?

God answers, calling the dreamer a precious child, and saying that they were never ever left alone. It was in those most troubled and painful times that the Divine carried the dreamer.

Divine persistence is perpetual, eternal, unending, undying, abiding, enduring, permanent, constant, unfailing, and never changing.

As you reflect on this chapter, continue to ponder. How have repeated lessons manifested in your life? Are there multiple scenarios or relationships that require the same challenge from you? What traditions are most meaningful in your life? Have you created beloved traditions from those things that repeat with resonance? How has God gotten your attention in important times? What ways has God used to get your attention that you are just realizing now?

*The use of they/their is intentional for including female/male pronouns.

PRESENCE *Recognizing the Divine in Your Everyday Life*

Concepts

Divine Persistence

Repeated lessons are a gift from God.

Repetition with Divine resonance becomes tradition.

Persistence is one of the many ways the Divine reveals itself.

God will use all available means to get our attention.

God's persistence is present even when we are unaware.

Chapter 4
Events Large and Small

No doubt you have watched movies in a theater or at home. Think of a movie and recall a scene that was particularly captivating or pivotal to the plot. The story told by the movie can have several significant events, such as a famous fight, a chase scene, or a chance meeting that sets two people off on a fantastic journey. There may even be a surprise ending.

William Shakespeare is believed to have written the phrase "All the world's a stage." Was he looking at our lives with their significant events that shape the plot of our story line? In some ways, our lives may be like movies, with us playing the main character. Like those productions, and like Shakespeare's stage, our life stories occasionally have scenes we can recall that stand out from what we otherwise experience as our regular lives.

Some events are out of the ordinary just because they are unique or at least rare, such as weddings, parties, date nights, speeches, unforgettable random experiences, performances, and brief encounters. Just as it is important to start looking for the meaning in things you might have not noticed before, events both large and small are rich sources of coming face-to-face with the Divine speaking and teaching.

Sometimes an event comes in a big box wrapped in beautiful paper and the tag has your name on it. Other events can be packaged in a box that is small, plain, or mundane. Either way, the contents can be extraordinary.

How can you be ready for the gift? Can you even recognize the gift when you receive it?

Some fairly recognizable indicators signal when an event involves a Divine intervention. It's so much more than just having a good time. It's more than making a good or bad memory. Divine interventions make the event transformative. After the event, you find yourself changed. You may also find yourself deeply moved or unable to shake a profound feeling that wasn't there before.

Just as a found piece of glass on a beach can be simply another piece of glass, you can instead be aware it is something provocative and meaningful to behold. A clue to the significance of the event may surface when you find yourself compelled to tell others of the experience with crystal clarity.

Divine interventions make an event transforming. You find yourself changed.
(Photo by Robert Els for Quechua Benefit)

62

Have you shared your experience of an event and discovered that the retelling brings the intensity of the emotional charge back as if it were still happening? That, my friends, is a clue that there is Divine mystery in the works, which prompts the recurring memory and the profound feeling that never leaves you.

Think of the attachment you may have had with a beloved pet that's passed away. Perhaps this happened a very long time ago. One day, you find yourself telling someone about the experience of the love you shared and the profound sadness in your loss. You become sad again in the telling. You feel the pain, and you fight back tears as if your pet died just yesterday.

That is the power of a Divine connection and presence. It differs from talking about a great concert you saw, an awesome movie you enjoyed, or fun you had at a party. Granted, those are all memorable and positive memories, but they don't have the same power of transformation.

Most of us remember our school years included times of awkwardness, self-discovery, self-loathing, doubt, and questioning. We get through those times in our school years, but most people never want to go back. Yet, inevitably, there will be a high school reunion. Each has its own hallmark. The 10th reunion is for seeing the product of your education and perhaps marriage. The 25th displays your career and family. It is the 50th that shows your life nakedly—who you became, your challenges, triumphs, and tragedies, and what life ended up looking like after the beautiful and handsome morphed into the ordinary, while the plain and unpopular in school sometimes took center stage in life.

For example, just about everyone says Dave is a nice person who's quiet and unassuming, never making waves for

63

himself or others. He doesn't think of himself as being very special. Most people, upon meeting him, find him exceptionally modest. It was out of character that he agreed to attend his 50th high school reunion. He hadn't been to any before that his small-town public school had held. Wanting to take his new romantic interest to an event, he chose to say yes and go. He had made excuses before even getting there, that it was likely that it would not be a big deal. He said he wouldn't remember most people and it was unlikely that anyone would remember him.

Dave entered the reception hall at the town center filled with what appeared to be aging strangers. Someone turned around and looked at him. After a second look and a quick glance at the name tag, the former classmate's face erupted with a smile of recognition, and he exclaimed, "Davy, oh my goodness! It's so good to see you. How are you? I can't believe it is you; what is going on with you?" The enthusiasm and energy were so strong and positive that Dave felt he was being greeted as a long-lost best friend. It practically bowled him over to have such a dynamic greeting. What a great beginning.

But that was only the beginning. The next person topped the first in his surprise and pleasure in seeing Dave. And the next and the next, until it became clear and overwhelming all through the night that so many people were overjoyed at seeing him and told him so. Through the night, Dave's whole demeanor changed, keeping pace with the wonderful responses. He smiled constantly, laughed, held his shoulders back and head high. He talked to nearly everyone, and he found time to sit with a couple of old friends and really connect.

64

By the end of the evening, Dave had transformed. Happy, excited, and feeling good, he finally expressed to his date, who was delighted to see his transformation, what he had been experiencing.

"I guess people really like me," Dave said.

For the evening, for the moment, Dave believed, breathed, and lived that he was treasured and beloved.

Isn't that what the Divine wants us to have, know, and feel? We are lifted up in the Light of a loving God to experience the sheer joy of existing and how our existence brings joy to others. But like Dave, we don't always know that. In fact, even if we catch a glimpse of it, as Dave did that night of his reunion, we sometimes forget it. When we discount that we are treasured and beloved for long enough, we begin denying it.

Then it becomes chronic, and we become more and more separated from the loved person we were created to be. We feel separated, until some event that is out of the ordinary leads us to be reunited with our true, divine self. It's not much of a stretch to connect the name of Dave's event, a *reunion*, with greater meaning and purpose. Was it not a deeper *re*-union with his true self, a *re*-union with God's love for Dave, a *re*-union with his original blessing as a child of God that was experienced as a result of this one night at this one event? We all have the potential for such an awakening in our lives.

What events—large or small—have filled you with that self-love, reflection, peace, tranquility, and confidence that may not be an experience you have ordinarily? Next time you have that experience, that feeling, that returns you to your true identity as a child of the Universe, loved and treasured, look for the deeper meaning in many of the details of the experience.

Some events are out of the ordinary just because they are unique or at least rare.
(Photos by Robert Els for Quechua Benefit)

No doubt, on this special night, Dave had a *reunion*, connecting with his experience of being loved, accepted, and celebrated. Weeks later, some of the photos taken were sent out. In the group photo of about 40 people, Dave stood in the front and center of the group, beaming. This is a man who, prior to the reunion, might well have chosen not to go. Had the group photo been taken early in the evening, he might have hidden away to the edge of the picture, behind others, perhaps only partially visible, with a forced expression only partially recognizable as a smile.

Instead, this was Dave's night to reclaim and rediscover who he really is and always has been. This experience of Dave's gives us the next concept, *God will use others to teach you.*

Here is a wonderful recounting of a much less formal event in which the Divine used others to send a clear message. Many years ago, Nancy was driving to a grocery store when she saw a woman, clearly in distress, standing beside her car with grocery bags on the ground. Nancy was drawn to stop and inquire if there was some way she could help.

"I went up to the woman and asked her what was wrong," Nancy recalled. "She told me she had been getting ready to put the groceries in her car when she, by accident, locked her keys in the car while it was running. Happy to help her, I took her and the groceries to the woman's home. She didn't live close, but it all worked out. I helped her in with the groceries, she got her extra set of keys, and off we went to return to the running car. Although it took some time, it wasn't that hard to do, and the woman was so grateful.

"The really interesting part of the story was what happened next," Nancy continued. "I went into the grocery store as I had originally intended. You know how people in a store aren't usually paying attention to you. They are busy with their grocery lists and operating in their own worlds. But not this day. From the time I walked into the store, people looked up at me. They smiled, warmly, nodding their heads in greeting. It was so different. It was not just a few people either, it was one person after another.

"Even telling the story now gives me chills," Nancy added. "It felt as though there was a physical connection, a tingling, and it was all so unexpected. I still remember it clearly these many years later. It was singular."

In this small event, the concept *God will use others to teach you* becomes clear when we see that the Divine was sending Nancy a clear message that what she had chosen to do (deciding to help the stranded women) was pleasing. The fact that Nancy had such a strong reaction to the people in the grocery store, not only at the time, but also in the retelling of the story, is an indication of God using others to send a clear message to Nancy of approval and gratitude for her actions.

Another experience of God seeming to speak with clarity happened on Kevin's first date with his wife of 30 years. While on their date, they started casual conversations twice with people they didn't know. What made it not so casual was that each time the other people asked the first-date couple the same question: "How long have you been together?"

For Kevin, it seemed such an odd question for strangers to ask, let alone for two people to ask the same question. But it wasn't just the question. When Kevin and his date said it was their first date, both times the other person responded, "You look like you have been together for a long time, like you belong together."

The fact that Kevin eventually married the woman from that first date, and they are together in a long-term marriage, gives even more meaning to those comments. In the telling of this story, Kevin said it seemed strange then, and even now it gives him a feeling of otherworldliness.

When we reflect on this event, can we hear the Divine speaking to Kevin and his date in a meaningful, encouraging, and prophetic way? That Kevin remembered such small incidents all these years later, and that it still gave him a special feeling, goes to the possibility that this was a mysterious encounter with Godly connection.

What about small events? How can something that might only last a few minutes, with no advance anticipation or invitation, also be a Divine intervention? Here is another real-life example of how what appears to be a random set of small actions can be profound. (That's how you know it is more than just ordinary.)

Meghan is a lovely person with a calm and considerate demeanor. Gentle spirited, soft spoken, and a reflective deep thinker, she looks at her own spiritual journey with curiosity. One day, we were having a conversation about spiritual thoughts and feelings.

"I have been thinking for days about something that happened to me about 20 years ago," Meghan said, after thinking quietly for a moment. "It keeps coming into my consciousness, so I guess I am supposed to share it with you.

"I was going to get gas in my car," Meghan continued. "The station was small and hard to navigate. It sold gas at a cheaper price than others in town, and people often stopped there for the convenience store as well. I maneuvered my car to the nearest pump and stopped in the spot behind the car ahead. Just as I came to a stop and momentarily got distracted looking for my credit card, the car in front of me left and a truck pulled up behind me. I looked in the rearview mirror to see the driver with an angry, disgusted expression. He put the truck in reverse just enough to give him room to back up and pull in front of me. As he passed me, he glared at me, cussing aloud through his open window, and shaking his fist with such force that the combination of his fierce expression, verbal ugliness, and aggressive fist shocked and scared me.

"I was so affected by this violent display that something came over me," Meghan added. "It was a feeling I rarely, if ever, have experienced, and that feeling compelled me to say and do something about it. My heart began to pound in my chest as I opened my door and left my car, heading toward the man in the truck. Even though it was just a few seconds' walk, I

69

must have had a hundred different scenarios pass through my mind as I approached him. At the moment our eyes met, a peaceful calm came over me, and I quietly said to him, 'You didn't need to have been so angry, or cuss at me, or do that with your fist.' In that brief eternity following what I said, he had no response—no words, no gestures, no twisted expression—and I returned to my car.

"I started the automatic ritual of filling up my car, but I watched as the man left his truck to go into the convenience store. He approached the door just as a couple of other people converged at the same time. I saw him stop and step aside as he politely opened the door with a smile and let the other people go ahead of him."

I listened to Meghan's story with a sense of the special event this was. Although the event lasted no more than five minutes, it was remembered for 20 years. Why would Meghan remember it all this time? And in such detail? Why, when we were exploring various spiritual themes, would this story surface so that she was compelled to tell it again?

Could Meghan have been an instrument of God in that man's life? Could she have been a messenger, so profound that in what could have been no more than a minute, he learned about kindness over cruelty, peace over rage, and compassion over toxic outrage? Perhaps some answers lie in the concept *God will use you to teach others a Divine message.*

Do you remember an experience, whether small or large, with such impact that it has stayed with you always? Did it have a profound effect on you? Perhaps on someone else?

When I see counseling clients, a phenomenon happens so often that it bears revealing. In the course of our helping and

70

healing relationship, it isn't unusual for me to offer a story or encouraging thought. I have a pretty good memory about themes or significant suggestions I've shared from session to session. In future sessions the person may refer to a previous conversation, saying, "I've been thinking about what you said last week. Remember when you said ___" and then they tell me a thought, attributed to me, that had a special meaning for them.

Wait! I never said that. Really, never. But the person vividly remembers, sometimes quotes, and goes on to say how meaningful, even life-changing, that story or thought was. I've learned not to disagree. I believe that what the person heard may have been a message meant for them from the Spirit which passes through all things, and as a counselor, I provided the environment in which it was heard.

At times I bring large and small events in my own life into the counseling session because they have personally affected me in such profound ways. A favorite experience I have often recalled is an example of when God used a small event from my everyday life to teach me. Though not immediately obvious, it became a gift to me that has helped me constantly. It has kept me going forward, especially helping me at times when I otherwise would have been stuck.

In my first job out of college, I lived in an old garden apartment that was plain, without modern conveniences, and set among the most unremarkable, dingy, unimaginative dwellings. My apartment was so low on the livable scale that even the laundry room, filled with coin-operated machines, was across the outside yard, in another building, and down the steps to a basement with unpainted concrete walls.

71

So, doing my laundry required a trip, sometimes in the dark after work, wearing a coat in cold weather, carrying an umbrella in the rain with my arms full of clothes. I often went down into that "laundry dungeon" only to find all the machines taken. So, I trudged back to my apartment to try again in the next hour, or the next day. It was dreadful.

After putting off doing laundry due to the horrible conditions, I realized something had to happen for me to break free from the intense resistance I felt to such a mundane, disgusting, but necessary chore.

One night, deep in my internal struggle, a question popped into my mind: "What *do* you have enough energy or motivation to do?"

I actually had an answer. I could search for the dimes (for drying) and quarters (for washing) I would eventually need and put them on the table by the door. Along with the question came a condition: I was to do nothing more than that.

Feeling satisfied, I went on to other matters. The next night, the same question and condition surfaced. I placed the detergent and fabric softener on the table by the door. The following night, I added the clothes. On the last night, I looked at the dimes and quarters, detergent, and clothes all waiting patiently for me to take them into my arms. I simply opened the door and took my first step on that seemingly long journey into the night to do my laundry.

That new routine repeated for each weekly laundry. Was my laundry preparation like a spiritual practice with the intentional ritual to prepare? With thoughtfulness, tasks may indeed become sacred.

Later, I applied the principle to other unmotivating tasks, then to daily to-dos, yearly plans, and life goals. I've told this story to many people. The principle keeps me unstuck and moving forward. I have used this technique ever

How can something that might only last a few minutes, with no advance anticipation or invitation, also be a Divine intervention?
(Photo by Robert Els for Quechua Benefit)

since, and I still remember the sense of movement I got from accomplishing the first difficult task of doing the laundry with renewed ability. I have since believed this supports the concept *God will enter your life as a teacher.*

Our lives contain large and small events that form the stories of our Earthly years. Perhaps the appeal of writings in books, plays, and movies comes from our seeking to learn through stories.

Many people read, study, and search the Bible for stories about events that are meant to guide them. Bible stories can teach us about the event and its lessons, and they can also show us how God wants us to learn about living in our own world.

Many people believe the Bible is the word of God. Why would we doubt that the events in our lives may also be the word of God manifest in our own experience? If God spoke to our ancient relatives depicted in the Bible, why can't God also

73

speak to us now? Could an event in your life be like a Bible story? That is certainly a provocative question to ponder.

Let's visit William Shakespeare's *As You Like It*, Act ll, Scene Vll, and continue with an adaptation of the often-quoted verse:

All the world's a stage,

And all the people merely players;

They have their exits and their entrances,

And each plays many parts.

If you think of your life as a play or a movie acted out on the stage of this world, you might recognize the players and scenes (events) as they pave your grand, artful, creative, unfolding life path. Could all the people be players, coming and going in your life, with a part to play that speaks a Divine message in your everyday life?

As you reflect on this chapter, continue to ponder. How has someone entered your life as a teacher? What lesson did you learn that was profound or that changed you? How have you entered someone's life as a teacher—perhaps unknowingly? What was it like to be the point of change and growth for that person? When has the Divine led you through an event, large or small, that set you forward on your spiritual and personal growth journey?

Concepts

Events Large and Small

God will use others to teach you.

God will use you to teach others a Divine message.

God will enter your life as a teacher.

Chapter 5
Simple Plans

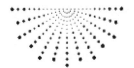

We have our plans. Sometimes they are clear and obvious and took much time and effort to develop. Other times they are assumed and unspoken. We love our plans because they give us an idea of what we want and how we are going to achieve our goals. So why do we find our plans disrupted so often? What does it mean to have plans change into the best or worst thing you could imagine or into something so different from your original plan?

Take a blank piece of paper and draw a straight line across it from edge to edge. Things that fall on this line are the normal kinds of life experiences that you have planned.

Let's define this line as your *okay line.* Write a few of your current life plans, which might include the following examples: continuing in the same job, running regular errands, going on a trip.

_____my okay line_____

When there is an abrupt change of plan, it may create a peak experience (whether positive or negative) that captures our attention. If drawn on this line, it may look like mountain peaks above and below the okay line.

my okay line

The high peaks would be the most positive experiences, such as having an unexpectedly fun-filled vacation after plans got ruined at the start or being admitted to a fabulous educational program after your first choice rejected you. Examples of the lows would be getting a divorce when you had planned a lifelong marriage or having a painful accident when you previously had ideal health.

We typically reflect on our peak experiences by recalling them many times, or recounting them often to our friends, maybe starting with a statement like, "You won't believe what happened to me the other day."

Those new plans teach us. We may remember them and wonder about them throughout our lives. Consider the happenings we find above (or below) that okay line that were unplanned and caused us to focus. Often the experience stands out because it interfered with other plans. Whether our plans are for a lifetime or just for today, something unexpected can change them in a moment, and that alerts us to consider the presence of the Divine.

A friend of mine had been working as a therapist for many years. She planned to be a therapist long into her future.

When she divorced, life and work became harder to balance. One of her male counseling clients began pursuing her, wanting her to date him, which is unethical in the profession. She had experienced so much stress in her job already that the unwanted attention became the straw that broke the camel's back. She decided she just didn't want to continue as a therapist.

Whether our plans are for a lifetime or just for today, something unexpected can change them in a moment, and that alerts us to consider the presence of the Divine.
(Photo by Robert Els for Quechua Benefit)

This disruption of her plan to work as a therapist—her client repeatedly asking to date her—put her over the edge, and she decided to walk away from a career she had invested in for decades. She went to work in another field, and that job led to something else. She eventually entered a different career, thrived, and enjoyed her work thereafter. No romantic relationship ever came from the guy wanting to date her, but that nudge changed her entire life plan.

When events, perhaps of no great consequence at the time, create an enormous change in your life, could that be a message from Spirit to move you off your current direction on

78

to another path? You might ask, "How is this different than just the idea that stuff happens, and why is this example a reflection of Divine activity?" It is the *outcome* that defines the difference between just stuff that happens (when the *outcome* remains on the okay line) and that which alerts you to the possible influence of the Divine. Notice when the *outcome* becomes a peak experience. That leads to the next concept, *Your plan may be supported or derailed by Divine influence.*

We can be going along with our simple plans. Sometimes someone's comment or advice can create profound change in our lives. Perhaps someone said something to you, once, a long time ago, that changed your plans forever.

One ordinary day, when I was about 13, my mom and I were alone in the kitchen while she was fixing dinner. I was sitting at the table engaged in some idle task. She began to talk about how I was doing poorly in school. She became very angry and upset with me.

"You will never do anything better than canning tuna in a tuna factory," she said.

Boy, did that sting, and it made me both sad and mad. That one comment changed me forever because I found myself determined to prove her wrong. I worked toward my potential no matter what. That one sentence, said in anger, when I was fairly young, set me on a new course of achievement for the rest of my life. I developed determination and tenacity that have carried me through many accomplishments because I would never give up on a goal. If I couldn't achieve it one way, I'd find another way.

Of course, it wasn't until after I achieved academic success that I came to realize that working in a tuna factory is as

79

valuable and noble as any job or any career. Over time, I learned that your importance doesn't come from the job you do, or how many degrees you have, but from the person you are and the caring heart you have. Some people may know this from the start of their lives, but I had to wage the uphill battle of achieving the academic accomplishments to show me that they didn't make me a better person. Being a loving and caring person is the life goal worth pursuing.

But for hardheaded me, it took the pain of the words and actions of first my mother and then a boyfriend, and finally my doing what I thought was necessary to become a worthy person. I finally understood the Divinely inspired truth of what is really important. That important truth lies in each one of us as we (and all others) understand that we are a product of original blessing. We are beloved and worthy simply because we are the children of God.

A wonderful true story shares experiences of a veterinarian who serves the pets of the homeless. Dr. Kwane Stewart had other plans for his career when he came upon a homeless person and his dog. Dr. Stewart describes it as "that one little moment" when his plans for his life suddenly changed. He also summarizes his transition to street veterinarian as, "it feels like it's home to me." I encourage you to search for *Today Show Street Veterinarian: Meet the 'street vet' treating pets of the homeless in his area* (https://www.today.com/video/meet-the-street-vet-treating-pets-of-the-homeless-in-his-area-96153157865) to see this tender, powerful story, showing how one encounter changed his and others' lives.

Do you think the Divine was with me during those hurtful times to influence me? You might ask why I have attributed what happened to Divine influence. Why were they not just

PRESENCE *Recognizing the Divine in Your Everyday Life*

human encounters that shaped my life course? I return to the idea of *outcomes*. I am sure I have had many unkind, unthinking things said to me that long ago became part of a larger backdrop on my okay line. Like water off a duck's back, like something quickly forgotten, not every difficult event rises to the level of these events I have just shared. These events made a difference in my life. I can recall them in detail and with emotion. In retrospect, they engaged a part of me that changed forever. God showed me the way, partnered with me through the experiences and the resulting changes, and helped heal the wounding pain from the experiences. Experiences like these support the next concept, *Divine influence is with you in the painful times.*

Let's look at two more examples of how God can use painful times when plans change to influence us toward growth. A counseling colleague of mine told me that one day, as a young girl, she was upset and crying.

"Don't feel that way," her father said. "You are *not* upset, so stop it."

She still remembers the traumatic impact of being told not to feel a certain way. She remembers feeling discounted. She carries that with her to focus on being protective about her own and others' feelings. She may not have planned to have that become a major focus in her adult life, but it did.

Her life plan supported the amazingly kind, empathetic way she now works with families. She credits that her father's hurtful comment was the turning point that led her to live by a life philosophy and choose a career based on respecting, honoring, and protecting feelings. Could a massive shift in self-perception and the resulting change in the trajectory of her life plan have been Divinely inspired?

81

For another example, a couple was struggling through marriage counseling. The husband could not attend one session, and the wife went by herself.

"Do you think he will ever change?" the counselor asked the wife.

The question hit her like a Mack truck. Upon reflection, knowing the answer was "no," the wife eventually decided to end the painful marriage.

That woman has now been remarried for more than 25 years to a loving, caring second husband. Her original plan was to be married to her first husband forever, and yet, just one question that would not have been asked had the husband been present changed the course of her life. Was the Divine in that room, guiding the counselor, caring for the woman, changing her plan?

I remember when I was working during the day and going to community college at night. Planning to continue on to work on my bachelor's degree, I was lamenting about how long it would take me to finish. I was dating Herbie, a very smart young man, who took out a piece of paper and showed me in writing how taking a school loan would actually save me money by getting me graduated and making a better salary faster than my plan "A." That one idea, taking probably no more than a few minutes, changed my future dramatically, because I took his advice.

When you look at these examples of plans being changed, or you consider similar experiences from your own life, do you wonder about God's will versus free (human) will? Is it you who are changing your plan? Or does the Divine play a part in the change? How would you connect the Divine with coincidence, luck, or predestination? Do God and luck work together?

Sometimes, life lessons come when we are just nudged in a direction. Sometimes if we don't learn our lesson the first

God showed me the way, partnered with me through the experiences and the resulting changes, and helped heal the wounding pain from the experiences.
(Photo by Robert Els for Quechua Benefit)

time, we get nudged again. Is that our free will? If that second lesson really shows the Divine is present in these things, what does that mean? Is your life direction all just random chaos, free will, or Divine intervention? How does the Spirit move in your life when your plans take an unexpected turn?

Much has been written and discussed about free will. At the simplest level, free will can be described as doing what we want, when we want, and how we want to do it. If I want cereal and milk for breakfast, given the necessary resources, I fix it and eat it. I don't pray for God's help or wait to feel the Spirit moving. I can use the same free will if I don't want to eat.

Sometimes our plans are more complicated than fixing breakfast, or they can *become* more complicated. When has that happened to you? When has something simple become a major shift in your life plan?

Coincidence is a phenomenon that most of us have experienced. Made up of the prefix "co" and the root word

83

"incidence," it generally happens when events occur at the same time by accident, without planning, but work out as though they were planned. Merriam-Webster dictionary states: "The occurrence of events that happen at the same time by accident but seem to have some connection."

Examples of coincidence include thinking of friends from long ago and running into them that very day in the most unusual settings, telephoning someone at the exact same time they call you, or encountering an unusual symbol or sign that speaks to a question or concern that has been on your mind.

What coincidences in your life made a major impact? If the Divine is always present, could a coincidence actually be part of the Divine mystery?

Remarkable coincidences make us think of other words and ideas such as: fate, accident, chance, destiny, synchronicity, law of cause and effect, happenstance, random, Divine intervention, and "everything happens for a reason."

How have any of these words or ideas played a part in your life? Has it ever crossed your mind that the hand of God could be at play?

Think of Bible stories that seem unlikely, such as the miracle stories or the encounters with unusual people. Would your most incredible life events be like a Bible experience in your own life story? Your stories may also seem unlikely or unusual, yet you know them to have actually happened.

Sometimes, despite all our plans, whether explicit or implicit, bad things happen. The okay line plummets to the bottom. How can the Divine be in that?

Some of that answer may be influenced by your belief in the nature of God. For example, if you believe God is like a

84

puppeteer who holds each and every string that controls your life, it might appear to you that God is making bad things happen to you on purpose. That purpose could be to punish you for something you thought, said, or did. Perhaps. Here is another possibility.

I use a powerful example from my everyday life. Many people like to call the Divine "Father," or some say "Father/Mother." Either way, God is often referred to as a parent. So, let's look at parenting as a possible way to understand the relationship the Divine has with each of us.

As a parent, I know I have influence over my children, but I really don't have any control, especially from the time they begin to make their own decisions. My duties, which I am grateful for, are to guide, care for, keep safe, provide opportunities, help educate, and, most of all, love them.

As my children grow and take on more responsibility for their decisions and actions, I have a pretty good idea when they are making mistakes—things that don't help them and that can cause them regret or pain. Most of the time, I assess the potential harm and act accordingly.

For example, if my two-year-old daughter reached for the handle on a pot of boiling water, I pushed her away even if it made her fall down and get upset with my abrupt and seemingly unprovoked action.

Sometimes I can't protect my children from harm, for example, when my child ran down the street, suddenly tripped and fell, scraping a knee. I couldn't prevent the fall, nor was I responsible for the fall.

Sometimes bad things happen just from the randomness of our Earthly existence combined with the arbitrary chaos of the

85

moment. Perhaps my child, usually so successful when running at high speed, was distracted and didn't land on her foot with the needed balance, or she didn't see the seam in the road surface that wasn't smooth. However, once she had fallen, bloodied her knee, and cried out in pain, I could take her in my arms, comfort her, be with her while she cries, give her healing medicine, perhaps teach her a lesson about being more careful, and help her find the confidence to run again another day.

Perhaps that is a good way for us to think of God, not as the puppeteer holding all the strings of your life, but as a loving and kind presence. The Divine may not have been the cause for the pain you feel but is there to hold and comfort you, and to help you heal and go out into the world again. This belief leads us to the concept *God does not cause bad things to happen, but comforts when they do.*

Many of us have had times when we have not accepted any comfort from the Divine or from our friends and family. There are times when we feel utterly forsaken. I have known those times, and yet, they haven't lasted forever. Sometimes it takes time in that painful place before we can open ourselves to comfort. Often when I see a new client, it is because they have reached the end of a painful and empty time and seek counseling as a last attempt. I always feel a powerful Divine presence in that first meeting, not because they believe it, but because I believe it. This is why kindness is so mighty. That Divine presence can be found in a kind word or deed from anyone at any time. You may never know what profound comfort you may offer someone who is in such pain.

Sometimes, despite all our plans, whether explicit or implicit, good things happen. Suddenly that line on the page is

86

way above the okay level. What is that about? How can the Divine be in that? Does God play a role in your being lucky?

One day, I decided to goof off with some fun, slightly crazy friends of mine about three hours from home. We were just starting one of those pleasant evenings over dinner when my phone rang, and I was informed that my seven-year-old grandson had fallen from the second story of the barn at my farm while with his grandfather. He had stepped toward the open area where we threw hay to the animals, placed his weight on a weakened board, and tumbled down onto a concrete pad. His grandfather picked him up, put him in the car, and drove him to the nearest emergency room.

Eventually I spoke to the ER doctor on the phone, who told me they suspected my grandson had broken his back. I called my daughter, his mother, and told her everything, and she hurried to the emergency room. You can imagine the fear, concern, and dread that I felt. It turned out that there was no fracture of any kind, no real injury in fact. The doctors concluded that he must have fallen on one of the animals resting below rather than the concrete. When retelling this story to friends, here were the comments I heard:

"Thank God."

"The Lord was with him."

"God saved him."

I wasn't convinced. I kept thinking about all the other little boys who had accidents like that who did break their backs, boys who were permanently injured, or died. Would people say:

"God caused that."

87

"God was absent."

"God didn't save him."

So, what does that say about the presence of the Divine when something good happens? Could it be

Does God take credit for the good things that happen?
(Photo by Robert Els for Quechua Benefit)

that accidents are the random results of us being careless or distracted? Is God there for the comfort but not the cause? Does God take credit for the good things that happen? I think this concept speaks more to what feels real: *The Spirit does not cause good things to happen but rejoices when they do.*

Let's look at a subtle but important difference between God not *causing* good or bad things to happen, and the Divine influence we have already spoken about that has the power to change the course of a life.

Some time ago, I had a major decision to make. One of my clients had unexpectedly become a guardian to two very young children long after raising and launching her adult children. She was struggling with the possibility of becoming an active parent as an older person with plans of her own.

Although I may informally suggest a book or a good acupuncturist to one of my clients, I am aware that I am not to

88

interfere in a *causal* way in my clients' lives—other than in safety or life-and-death issues. I had a dilemma: I knew of a couple who had taken on foster children very successfully in the past. Would I, could I, should I connect these people—one a client, the other friends?

After much reflection, I considered the difference between being one who *caused* something versus someone who *influenced*. If ethically done, my introduction of the guardian and the potential foster would not *cause* an outcome, but it surely might be an influence in many people's lives.

We are always influencing one another, so after great consideration, I felt it was not inappropriate for me to introduce information—even if it might be influential. Whether the connection resulted in any changes in those lives was not something I directed or caused. That is how I view the difference between the Divine being an influence in our life when we learn and grow from our experiences as opposed to the Divine being the cause of good or bad.

I hope that helps to understand the subtle but important difference between a God who causes events by judging who gets the goodies and who doesn't and a God who influences by presenting opportunities. In this case, once introductions between the guardian and the potential foster were done within professional and ethical guidelines, I retreated from any involvement. This is a story that had a happily-ever-after ending, but not because I caused it.

The concept of predestination can also surface when thinking of life plans. Does God have a predestined plan for our lives and are we on Earth to discover and fulfill it? Merriam-Webster defines predestination as, "The doctrine that God [having] foreknowledge of all events infallibly

89

guides those who are destined for salvation." Explanations of predestination often seek to address the paradox of free will. But I would offer some other considerations. Is the Divine a maker of your future, or a partner in it?

When you become the planner of your calendar and you run into things that just won't work no matter how you try, is it because your path has been predestined? Or is God perhaps acting as teacher and counselor to get you to a better place on your path? What happens if you listen and change your life plan? What happens if you get the message but do something else? Or what happens when you have plans, and they just fall apart? What happens when those plans open up?

Let's look again at a story, first told as a favorite thing in Chapter 2. This is an example of how a significant time in your life can reflect multiple concepts. With a second look at this story, we can see the effect of the concept *Your plan may be supported or derailed by Divine influence.*

My entrance into pastoral counseling was more remarkable than one might have expected. I had become desperately disillusioned in a profession I had previously loved. I am fond of saying, "The gum had lost its flavor."

After a massive downsizing in my work organization, I was asked to design and conduct a weeklong training for the people who had been notified of losing their jobs. Having the opportunity to help those people who were in such a vulnerable and painful place transformed me. It touched a place inside my soul that sprang alive for the first time in my life. I knew there was a path for me that was different than the one I was on.

Although I kept my employment, I was affected by the reorganization following the downsizing, and I was given a new position. I really hated the new position.

So, I began considering a change of careers and becoming a counselor. A friend suggested the Loyola Pastoral Counseling program to me. Although the program was appealing in every way, I couldn't imagine I could ever be a pastoral counselor. But I was willing to try.

Before long, I left that job. As a single parent raising two- and four-year-old daughters, I began as a graduate student at midlife.

My transition to become a student under these unusual conditions was made only after many conversations with the Divine. I had talks about whether I was worthy and had what it takes to be a counselor. I wrestled with the decision. It was definitely appealing to consider being a counselor, but it looked like such a hard path to walk when I had such heavy responsibilities in my life. I dismissed the idea of going back to school many times, and many times the idea just kept alive.

Finally, rather than continuing to wrestle with what seemed to be a Divinely inspired step on my path, I decided to propose a deal to God. I know, that sounds so terribly arrogant, but I was desperate, and you know desperate people do desperate things! So, I proposed my bargain to my dear, loving, kind, understanding, and infinitely patient God.

I made a commitment to God that I would pledge going forward if the doors were opened. I promised I would take one step at a time. I also promised that if I found a brick wall on the path, that I would not beat myself up hitting that wall over and over, but I would turn to another direction if it

91

appeared this was not the path for me. And with my commitment, I began one of the most wonderful experiences of my life as a student in pastoral counseling. So began my plan and my passion.

After several very successful semesters, all the open doors suddenly appeared to close, and that brick wall appeared. I couldn't afford financially to continue my classes.

I had volunteered to work registration. When the time for registering was near closing, my favorite professor, who was volunteering next to me (coincidence?), said for me to do my own registration. I told her I wasn't going to school this semester because I didn't have the money.

She scribbled a note on a sheet of paper and gave it to me, directing me to go see the financial person, who was NEVER in her office. So I went, and to my surprise, she was there. She asked if I could wait. Her question made me laugh—like I had so much to do! Within a couple of minutes, she came out with a typed form and told me to go see the dean, who also was also NEVER in his office, to get his signature.

Well, the dean was in his office that day. I asked if he had a minute to look at the paper.

"How much do you need?" he asked.

I thought he was kidding. I mumbled that I needed tuition.

"What about books?" he asked. "Don't you need money to buy books and supplies?"

He wrote a sum of money on the blank line on the page that covered everything. Within 20 minutes, I went from having no money and having plans to skip a semester to having everything I needed and more.

92

I guess that closed door wasn't really closed, was it?

Could it all have been coincidences that, when put together, became a loud, interrupting force in my plan to step off my path? I felt the hand of God on my back pushing me back on my path, back on to the plan that I had committed to, the plan that I said I would step forward on *if the door opened.*

As you reflect on this chapter, continue to ponder. Have your plans been sidetracked? Derailed? Blocked? Can you trace the outcome of those actions and see a greater purpose? In your lowest times, have there been signs of a caring and concerned Presence with you, even if you rejected it at the time? When bad things happen, have you seen the hand of God reach out in comfort? When good things happen, how is the joy lifted and multiplied?

Concepts

Simple Plans

Your plan may be supported or derailed by Divine influence.

Divine influence is with you in the painful times.

God does not cause bad things to happen but comforts when they do.

The Spirit does not cause good things to happen but rejoices when they do.

93

PART II

DIVINE PRESENCE IN THOUGHT AND WORD

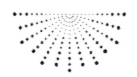

Chapter 6
The Split of the Spiritual Condition

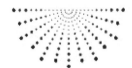

In *Part I, Encountering Divine Presence,* we have seen how encountering the Divine takes mindfulness to realize what is present every day in our lives. The discovery may unfold in our lives as the joy of our favorites, as persistent patterns, in events large and small, and in our plans and actions. We have considered concepts that explore the mystery of God. How else does the Divine manifest in our lives? Could it be our life experiences in an ongoing way but perhaps we never paid attention?

In *Part II, Divine Presence in Thought and Word,* we will explore ideas deeply that form a foundation of spiritual philosophy and theory. We will shed light (Light?) on our spiritual condition. From there, we will explore the language we use to communicate with the Divine. Words will transform to become symbols of our thoughts and feelings. Those words will then shape our most treasured stories. Finally, we will look at our connection with the Divine through the legends we live in our own lives.

96

We begin by considering the most basic aspect of our spiritual condition. As flesh-and-blood humans, we delight in what we can think, perceive, create, and ponder. Our point of view helps

Being split in our spiritual condition results in being of two minds.
(Photo by Katie Safley for Quechua Benefit)

define how we understand our world and our relationships.

What is it about our spiritual condition that compels humans to feel pulled toward something that we often cannot quite define or understand? Consider this interpretation. Perhaps we are constantly striving to heal ourselves due to our being split or broken in our *spiritual* condition, and the pull we feel is toward the path to Wholeness or Oneness with the Divine.

The theme of the conflict is constant. It is within us and separates the part that connects us with the Divine from the part that sets its course away from God. This theme runs like a river through much of the literature we treasure. It can even be found at the beginning of the Bible.

The narrative of the Garden of Eden is the first symbolic story of living humans in the Bible. This garden and its one

97

human,[1] whole and pure, are fully connected to the Divine. This fully formed human (male and female together) is able to partake of the original blessing in the garden without conflict or question. Yet this ideal original blessing is disrupted by the many splits to come: the split of female and male, the split of the original blessing from what the serpent was offering, and later the split of Cain and Abel.

Could our conflict be our inheritance from the symbolic Adam and Eve whose choice to hide from God established the path away from God?

Surely, the constant splitting creates with it more and more of what we may eventually consider human chaos. Splitting also leads to the battle within us as we put people in the category of "other," apart from ourselves, thereby splitting in every way that we can conjure. This "othering" leads to our many ways of fearing and then trying to control those we perceive as different from ourselves.

Being split in our *spiritual* condition results in being of two minds: Out of our fear and sense of scarcity comes *the mind for the individual*, and out of our connection with love and a sense of abundance comes *the mind for God*.

The *mind for the individual* is recognizable as it manifests in self-serving motives, self-centeredness, dread, control, meanness, deceit, an atmosphere of insufficiency, and many

---

1 The first two chapters of Genesis have competing stories of creation. Chapter one has God making man and woman simultaneously. The two would have been in the Garden of Eden from the beginning. The second chapter has man being created first and woman being formed from a rib, coming second and later.

PRESENCE *Recognizing the Divine in Your Everyday Life*

more effects of being separated from the Divine. We strive to rid ourselves of the powerful influence this part has over us.

The *mind for God* is based in love, freedom, empathy, kindness, truth, inclusion, and many more effects of being fully connected to the Divine. The *mind for God* believes we are surrounded with plenty. It is manifested when we feel awe, beauty, gratitude, humor, generosity, and thankfulness. It often is experienced most profoundly during the transitions of birth, death, and healing.

The part of our spiritual condition called the "mind for the individual" is the part of us that is concerned with how we look, our worry about the status of our jobs, how much money we have, and our day-to-day fears about how to survive. It is the part of us that sees itself as separate, special, individual, and apart from everything else. It is "me versus other." It thinks it knows the truth and does not hesitate to say so. It commands so much of our attention that we hardly recognize a conflict. We are simply too busy to hear a still small voice calling from what seems to be an almost imperceptible inner reservoir.

This "mind for the individual" is part of our *spiritual condition.* We shall use a shortened form and call it iMind. Our iMind is sometimes so successful and persuasive that we tend to forget the other mind, the "mind for God." Sometimes our conflicts with others' iMinds keep us quite occupied.

Certainly, iMind has carried us far through its inventiveness and logical understandings. We have solved economic problems and raised living standards through much of the world. Yet for so many people who live in poverty and who are food insecure, economic woes remain. Serious illnesses have been brought under control. Yet new diseases create themselves while ancient ones, like cancer, continue. We have

99

created amazing labor-saving and mobility-enhancing devices. Paradoxically, higher proportions of us work longer to pay for labor-saving devices. Despite the iMind's victories, solutions to major problems defy our best efforts. The ozone layer weakens while hurricanes grow more numerous and more destructive. People do not seem to grow less angry. Peace seems temporary or just beyond reach.

The other part of us that experiences joy, appreciates beauty, loves music, and feels connected to everything (even if only for a while) comes from the "mind for God." This is our true self, and it opens into our lifelong core identity as a beloved child of God. It taps into the inner reservoir, our soul. We know it when we experience it in our relationship with the Divine, and with the Divine in others.

As I mentioned in the beginning of this book, I have embraced the Quaker faith and practice description of the connection with God by recognizing the Spirit in all people. That experience is spoken of as seeking "that of God in everyone." Quakers also use the metaphor of Light to refer to the Divine. They often speak of the Light within, or the Light of the Divine that pours out into the world. When praying for someone, they "hold them in the Light." That Light is both constant and inclusive, and it speaks to and with the mind for God. We shall use a shortened form of the mind for God and call it gMind.

I read a few favorite written prayers. (Most of my prayers are either conversations between me and God or Jesus or holding someone in the Light.) One is what is widely known as the Prayer of St. Francis. The research often disputes whether it was really written by St. Francis of Assisi, but I don't find

100

where it came from that important. Here is the written version I like best:

Make me an instrument of your peace,
Where there is hatred, let me sow love;
Where there is injury, pardon;
Where there is doubt, faith;
Where there is despair, hope;
Where there is darkness, light;
Where there is sadness, joy.

O Divine One,
Grant that I may not so much seek
To be consoled as to console;
To be understood as to understand;
To be loved as to love.

For it is in giving that we receive;
It is in pardoning that we are pardoned;
And it is in dying that we are born to eternal life. Amen

Here is a closer look at this favorite prayer through the lens of our split spiritual condition. This prayer is a striking example of both iMind and gMind. Let's look at the wisdom revealed.

Make me an instrument of your peace. The opening line asks for us to become an instrument of God, an extension and example of God's teachings. In Chapter 4, Events Large and Small, we explored the idea that God will use your life as a teacher. This concept goes beyond being made in the image of God to being used by God to fulfill a holy purpose.

What an amazing and powerful idea that we can connect so closely with the Divine that we can transform ourselves and our world as the Divine has intended.

101

We can connect so closely with the Divine that we can transform ourselves and our world as the Divine has intended.
(Photo by Katie Safley for Quechua Benefit)

The prayer asks us to first bring *peace*. Peace and love are the foundations of gMind. Love is the thought and intention; peace is the outcome. If you find you are thinking and acting from a place that embodies peace, it is likely that you are in the spiritual condition of gMind. The iMind, on the other hand, comes from a place of fear. It experiences anger and embraces the philosophy of scarcity. It drives the human response to become defensive and protective.

Where there is hatred, let me sow love. Is your heart full of love, and therefore connected to the Divine? How often have you found yourself steeped in love for someone, or for a concept, or a hope? There is so much to love in our lives, and we can focus on those important parts of our lives and find them in the lives of everyone.

If you are looking for a guide for the direction of your path, consider asking yourself the question, "Am I doing this to sow seeds of love?" If you are, you are joining your gMind. Hate is the driver of cruelty, control, and meanness. It is quite clear when you are in that place of iMind. Awareness of what leads to your acts of cruelty, control, and meanness is the first step in stopping hatred.

We often hear the saying "God is Love." Many Western-culture religions use the Bible's 10 Commandments as the foundational guides to belief and behavior. In Christian writings, Jesus emphasized only two Commandments, saying they embodied everything we needed for our way of living together (the law) and our understanding of ourselves and others (the prophets.) Those greatest two Commandments are: Love God with all your heart and mind, and love your neighbor as you love yourself.

To sow love within ourselves and among our neighbors includes all people, thereby promoting anti-racism and anti-sexism and eliminating all forms of prejudice throughout the world. We come to know sowing love is the goal of our path, the way toward wholeness, and the work of the gMind.

Where there is injury, pardon. Hurt, suffering, pain, and hopelessness arise from the chaos of our human condition. Sometimes these realities seem to be everywhere. If we spread them in our thoughts, words, or actions, we are collaborating with our iMind to grab at what we desire without any thought of how that may affect someone else. That comes from a place without empathy and of indifference to the negative effect of our choices.

The irony is that spreading negativity becomes the source of our own pain as well. Pardon is forgiveness and grace. To

103

forgive others and forgive ourselves is to be fully connected to our gMind. We feel the love, kindness, and openness of the blessing of Spirit. When we forgive our neighbor, we are truly the instrument of God. When we forgive ourselves, we partner with the Divine in defining our creation as something that was manifest in love. God's love reveals the original blessing. The powerful parable of the Prodigal Son brings the gift of pardon and forgiveness to life.

In the large scale, injury is the outcome of racism, sexism, and other separations we create here on Earth. In separation, one is typically deemed superior to another. It seems so obvious that separation and the injury accompanying it go against all the best that we could experience at the human level. How could we kill, enslave, deny rights, imprison unjustly, and create a culture in which superiority and inferiority (iMind concepts) become the measure of the way we live? Often, we don't even recognize it. That is the deceit of the iMind.

Where there is doubt, faith. Doubt, suspicion, lies, and deception eat at the core of our souls. It is doubt that the iMind feeds on to focus on ourselves as individuals without care or concern about the welfare of anyone else. We can also find ourselves falling into a downward spiral of our own internal pain and depression.

Embracing faith is such an enlightened way to combat doubt. Our connection to God is direct and strong where there is faith. Our gMind is alive and unstoppable when buoyed by our trust, belief, and commitment.

Even though we trust that faith can promote more goodness than doubt, I wonder if doubt is ever healthy? Can doubt create space for transformed faith and strengthen our faith?

104

In my counseling office, I display a few of my favorite sayings, hoping they will inspire my clients as they have inspired me. One of my favorites is, "What would you accomplish if you knew you could not fail?" That saying speaks to what I believe faith gives us, because it is the mind of God that turns us toward love and away from fear. Knowing we do not have to fear gives us a way to open ourselves to growth.

I have a client who experienced severe emotional trauma in his childhood. As a middle-aged professional, he is aware of how much he dislikes the profession he has worked in for more than 20 years. What holds him back is his fear that he will not succeed if he tries something else. I asked him to shift his perspective: Instead of defining success as becoming accomplished in a newly tried field, I asked him to consider defining success as exploring the mystery of a new field. Surely, he will learn new things about himself and the world. Those new things may open other doors. The success he seeks will be in the discovery of all of this new experience and information. As he finds himself enjoying these discoveries, with that perspective, success is almost inevitable. As he overcomes his doubt, he will develop his faith.

Where there is despair, hope. To fall into the state of despair is to turn your back on the presence of the Divine in your life. Despair is the home of the iMind. It is empty and false and and prepares conditions for the iMind to feed the individual in ways that are both self-centered and selfish. Hope is the healing balm to the pain in our world. Hope gives us a positive vision, focus, and direction as we take our next step on our path. Our gMind thrives on hope because it is the energy of goodness and love.

And yet, hope is a tricky idea. There is false hope. Consider being in a relationship for a long time where the other person is abusive, disrespectful, and controlling. It is false hope to rely on the perpetrator suddenly turning around.

I know that experience all too personally. I lived in that false hope for many years before realizing that the true hope, that which was from the mind for God, was in the love and support available for me to stop participating in that toxic life. Where there was despair, there was also hope. Sometimes that hope exists in places where it is not always expected or obvious.

Where there is darkness, light. The concept of darkness represents the absence of all that is good and Godly. All our literature, images, and metaphors convey the symbolic idea of darkness as that which is bad, wrong, and evil. And yet, there is darkness that is peaceful and serene. When we close our eyes to shut out the light, we rest. When night falls, our world sleeps and renews, and we see the moon and stars that light up our sky. Our worldwide sisters and brothers are all beloved children of God, and yet we come in all hues, light to dark. Yet that variation of color is not an indication of either badness or goodness. Where that erroneous connection is made, we have racism with all its horror and ugliness as consequences for both victim and perpetrator.

When we look at the color of flowers, we often see the darkest color as the most beautiful, and sometimes whiteness can symbolize the most fearful, as in a great white shark. This part of the prayer is a very precise reference that speaks to that which is the mind for the individual versus the mind for God. This specific darkness is the emptiness of goodness that the iMind seeks as a dwelling place. Ask yourself why this may be.

Within this dark place, the iMind can work its process of feeding the self-indulgent needs and wants for me, myself, and I, without regard for the whole. The gMind brings the light of enlightenment to embrace the love of God for the reunification of the whole. Imagine the darkness of our world being replaced with light. How have the darkest places in your life been infused with Light?

Where there is sadness, joy. Happiness is the natural state of our original blessing. The concept from the chapter Favorite Things speaks of joy and how it is a gift from the Divine. *God wants all good for you.* Yet, to go into the world of sadness doesn't take a long journey. The chaos of our world and the split nature of our spiritual condition cause us to sometimes experience loss, sadness, and tragedy.

When our closest friends and relatives suffer, we seek to bring them back into the world of joy. When we are sad, we long for relief from the pain. Our own sadness is woven into the tapestry of our lives. Our sadness is like a huge rope, especially when it is new. It is heavy, overwhelming, and ever-present. Although the sadness remains in our memory, the heavy rope changes to become a single thread in our tapestry, giving the pattern of our fabric more depth and meaning. Joy, often referred to as the silver lining in the cloud, is also present.

In this Prayer of St. Francis, the plea is to be a giver of joy when finding sadness. We have developed entire psychologies and philosophies rooted in changing our perception from negative to positive, from sadness to joy. Our social justice efforts and charities follow in the same direction. We can be the givers of joy in micro ways and in massive ways. The intent

Once we let go of those things that hold us back from uniting with the Divine right now, our Earthly existence becomes our paradise.
(Photo by Katie Safley for Quechua Benefit)

is the same. Engaging our mind for God leads us to joy and to be the givers of more joy.

Not to be consoled, but to console. Not to be understood, but to understand. Not to be loved, but to love. In this part of the prayer, the focus shifts to give us the essence of the iMind versus the gMind. It expresses the empty demand for self-fulfillment of the mind for the individual being replaced with the loving, giving, wholeness of the mind for God.

When I encounter counseling clients who have suffered much tragedy in their lives, I ask them about the greatest hurt they have experienced. It is in defining their pain that recovery lives. It is a never-ending abyss to live in what you believe is the loss and pain in your life. It leads only to more heartbreak. To fill that void with what you have missed is healing. If you agonize in loneliness, visit a prisoner; if you crave to have your story heard, practice amazing listening; if you feel unloved, love all. If you live in, for, and through your iMind, open to your gMind, open to recognizing the presence of the Divine in your everyday life.

In giving, we receive. In pardoning, we pardon. In dying, we are born to eternal life. The final revelation of the prayer

108

supports the paradox of giving what you lack to receive it. It also adds to the ultimate contradiction of many religions—that what we seek here on Earth is available only when we leave our human bodies. The irony is that it is truly possible to experience the gifts of eternal life while we are in our human bodies. Once we let go of those things that hold us back from uniting with the Divine right now, our Earthly existence becomes our paradise.

As you reflect on this chapter, continue to ponder. How do you encounter iMind and gMind in your experiences? How does that split spiritual condition manifest in your life? Can you tell when you are experiencing one versus the other? Can you tell in your conscious and subconscious, your dreams, your gut feelings? Can you tell during remorse, joy, or prayer? Can you feel it in your body as your heart takes on different sensations, or as you feel comfortable or uncomfortable in your own skin? Do you see it in the congruence or incongruence of your spoken beliefs and your behavior?

Chapter 7
Exploring God in Our Words

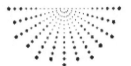

Many Christian cultures call the Bible "the word of God" or "the good Word." The Gospel of John speaks of the Word being Jesus:

> In the beginning was the Word, and the Word was with God, and the Word was God. (<u>King James Translation</u>)

> In the beginning the Word already existed; the Word was with God, and the Word was God. (<u>Good News Translation</u>)

Most of the thousands of languages spoken on Earth are made up of words. Those words express what we think, and they connect us to one another. Words can convey meaning, feelings, and information. Sometimes the words we choose are both powerful and deeply moving. They stand in for our emotions because they represent our feelings. We express both our mind for the individual (iMind) and our mind for God (gMind) in our spoken and written language.

In the split of our spiritual condition, we may find ourselves striving to connect to the Divine through our words, or we may use our words to protect the me, myself, and I of our iMinds. It's commonly said that "words matter."

We have been given the gift of language, and therefore we are responsible for becoming stewards of its use. We come into contact with words throughout the day, every day, and it follows to explore the deeper, symbolic meaning in a way that is similar to how we learned the dictionary meaning of those words. We can also explore them as we did in Part I of PRESENCE, seeking what has always been present but perhaps not fully noticed before.

No matter what language you learn, you begin with the individual word. From a word comes meaning. Our words develop into beloved and long-cherished poems, nursery rhymes, tales, legends, fairy tales, and books as they tell of powerful experiences and explore the mysteries of our lives.

Just as there are stories in the Bible full of symbols and meaning, there are stories full of symbolism in your own life. We have already looked at stories in Part I. Because the symbolism of words and stories speaks to our spiritual condition, they can be both personal and universal. We can also attempt to discern whether a word is more closely associated as a symbol of the mind for the individual (iMind) or of the mind for God (gMind).

Let's look at two examples of simple words that come to life when we look more deeply into the symbolic language that is beyond our literal minds.

111

Words express what we think, and they connect us to one another.
(Photo by Robert Els for Quechua Benefit)

Water: Let's look at a common word that is highly symbolic: water. We first want to look at words in a very broad way, using each in broader meaning. Water can evoke images like ocean, lake, river, still water, rain, and drinking water. The idea of water can be broad, an entire idea, arousing a whole array of meanings, even emotions.

Think of the amazing features of water: It covers the vast majority of our Earth, and it constitutes the vast majority of our human bodies. Because it is essential for our lives, we have to replenish our bodies with it constantly. Natural sciences tell us that life on Earth began in the water. So, we have an image of a life-giving, life-sustaining, life-creating force.

The image of water is often associated with the Divine itself. Jesus called the disciples from the water, walked on water, baptized with water, and turned water into wine. Various forms of water, especially large, powerful bodies of water, such as the ocean, are associated with our Spiritual Source, Sustenance, and Divine Presence (gMind). How do we handle the knowledge that water also floods and drowns?

112

Apple: Let's look at a word for a fairly ordinary item: apple. Literature and common sayings abound with apples. First, look at the obvious references that leap to our consciousness. "A" is for apple. A = beginning. Think of how many apples are famous: the apple in the Garden of Eden. (Yet, with careful reading of the King James version, it never says "apple." It says "fruit," but our culture and our collective intuition make it an apple.) Adam's apple is an outward sign of humanity and gender. Snow White ate a poison apple. William Tell shot an apple off his son's head. Isaac Newton's falling apple revealed the concept of gravity. An apple a day keeps (the doctor away) you healthy. We even call New York City—what some people consider the most important city in the world—the Big Apple. There is always the ideal gift for the teacher—the apple! What name was chosen for the breakthrough computers that transformed our daily world? Apple.

The symbol of an apple often indicates a separation from the Divine. Adam eating the apple separated him from God, Snow White ate the apple and "died." The teacher (and the gift of the apple) can be about rules and judgment, thereby separating us from God (iMind). Even the giver of the apple, the student who wants special favors or attention, is seen negatively by the other classmates.

The overwhelming experience of the word of God is that it is figurative. Yet, many of the ways we have experienced religion has been quite literal, as if that makes a word or story more factual. I wonder if by making it literal it makes it *less* factual? There is abundant, important reason for this. That which is symbolic touches both our thoughts and feelings. Comprehending that symbolic meaning requires work on our part because it is not spoon-fed as "fact" but given as a gift for us to experience and understand.

113

Meaning also expands beyond the limits of language. The use of words can be fluid due to culture, geography, generations, and circumstances. Culture grows organically, and the words that accompany it are bonded to that culture. Therefore, I acknowledge that the symbolism I propose is entirely connected to my gender, race, religious affiliation, and life experiences, some of which you share with me, and some you don't simply because we are people with two different life experiences. The wonderous aspect of this important reality is that no matter what culture a person comes from, deeper symbolic meanings are always relevant to her or his culture.

I am not an expert in language or symbols, so I am in the process of discovering meaning along with you. The following list of words with their accompanying symbolic meaning is an attempt to understand some of the more common symbols we encounter in our life experiences. It is not guaranteed accurate, nor is it complete. I ask you to add to it as you consider your own understanding of the many symbols in your life. Consider the transition from the literal meaning of words into their becoming symbols that we discover in our stories, poems, nursery rhymes, fairy tales, real-life experiences, and dreams. Rely on your intuition, perception, and understanding that the Divine will appear to you in ways that only you recognize.

Words and Their Symbolic Meanings

Objects and Things

1. Apple: our separation from God

2. Cars, trucks, trains, planes, boats: our spiritual journeys

3. Harp: connecting with angels, the Divine

114

4. Mirror: a true reflection

5. Phones: messages from the Divine

6. Snow: purity

7. Stairs, paths, and roads: the Spiritual journey

8. Stone: enduring truth of the Divine's promise and presence

9. Table: a higher understanding of Spiritual understanding

10. Treasure: the Divine

11. Well: our inner reservoir

People

12. Children: our imaginative, intuitive, and spiritual center that knows how to laugh and play

13. Giants, monsters, dragons: part not connected to good or God. Greedy, slow-witted, huge, dangerous, physically strong, but mentally and spiritually weak

14. Hunter: the one who sees clearly and whose aim is always true

15. King, prince: stand-in (in fairy tales) for the Divine

16. Mary, Virgin Mary: purity, vessel holding the Divine

17. Stepmother: Vanity, insecurity, not connected to good or God

18. Teacher (Outward): pay attention to the outward, separate ourselves from our tranquil inner place, our imagination, spiritual center, follow the rules, behave, judgmental and restrictive (iMind)

115

19. Teacher (Inner): intuitive where the Divine dwells within and spiritual learning and growth take place. When connected to God, we find we are guided by a faithful and devoted inner teacher (gMind)

Animals

20. Dove: peace, connects Earth and heaven (gMind)

21. Fish: evokes Jesus calling to the fishermen, the loaves and fishes, a symbol of Jesus and his followers

22. Lamb: Lamb of God refers to Jesus, the Christ Spirit

23. Wolf: the deceiver (iMind)

Places

24. Forests and deserts: wilderness, a disorienting state of mind, a god-forsaken place

25. Grocery store/market, restaurant: where we receive nourishment for our soul, food (like God's presence) feeds us and keeps us alive, sustenance

26. Hill, mound, mountain: represents a higher level of spiritual understanding than the ground

27. Home: dwelling with the Divine

28. House: the psychic space you occupy

29. Ocean: spiritual Source, the Divine, the mind of God (gMind)

30. Rivers: tributaries flowing toward and into the Divine

116

31. School (the outer school—iMind): where we are taught that reality is outside of us. We break the rules if we focus inward

32. School (the inner school—gMind): the inner sanctuary where connection, experience, and growth occur

Conditions

33. Death, sleep: separated from the ever-present and available inward reservoir of the Divine

34. Fasting: the preparation of emptying to be ready for a spiritual trial or enlightenment

35. Happily ever after: home (to Heaven) and fully connected with God

36. Hunger: emptiness longing to be filled with Divine nourishment and sustenance

37. Poverty: a spiritual condition based on a belief in the scarcity of God's unconditional love

38. Storms, battles, war: our turbulence as the iMind struggles with the gMind

Numbers

(Note: more likely to describe conditions than quantities.)

39. One, 1: unity, in unity with the Divine

40. Three, 3: connects parts so they become one. Divine wholeness, completeness, and perfection. If there ever was a desire to highlight an idea, thought, event, or noteworthy figure in the Bible for their prominence, the number 3 was used to put a Divine

117

stamp of completion or fulfillment on the subject. The Trinity, three wishes. It is a prime number, forms a triangle, and is the smallest number to form a pattern.

41. Four, 4: a number of completion—a sum of attributes connecting us to the Earth. Four points of the compass, the four seasons, four Earthly elements: Earth, Water, Air, and Fire. Four rivers flowing from the Garden of Eden.

42. Seven, 7: the antenna for God. It is shaped like an antenna, the shepherd's crook, or in the shape of a fishhook. It indicates perfection and completeness and is related to inner wisdom, mysticism, intuition, and inner strength. The seven dwarves, seven Chakras, seven seas, seven days of the week, seven continents.

43. Forty, 40: transition, gaining wisdom, level of maturity. A really long time. Example: turning 40, Biblical waiting of 40 days and 40 nights, Moses and the Israelis in the desert for 40 years, Elijah, Moses, and Jesus all fasted 40 days, 40 years from the crucifixion of Jesus to the destruction of Jerusalem, 40 days of Moses on the Mount receiving the Law, Moses's life being divided into three sections of 40 years, Noah's flood lasted 40 days and 40 nights, then waited 40 days after landing on a dry mountaintop before sending out a dove.

Directions

44. Left: the separate, weaker, directive side (iMind)

45. Right: Right is the spiritual side. The right brain is the creative side. John 21:6: "Throw your net on the right side of the boat and you will find some [fish]" (gMind).

46. North, South, East, West: Some say destruction and disaster come from the North. East is seen as an awakening, a vision, ascension. The Light rises in the East. West can symbolize a journey. Or the end of one phase of life. It is where the Light sets. The South can sometimes represent things going wrong, "going South."

Colors

(Note: I totally reject any racial connotations for the symbolism for the colors white and black. There is false reasoning for the choosing of these terms to designate race.)

47. White: purity, innocence, sacred (gMind)

48. Black: emptiness, receptive, negative (iMind)

49. Purple: royal, the established clergy

50. Yellow/sun: the Light of the Divine

51. Red: life, blood, human

This list of words is just a guide to open up your understanding, showing that words have deeper meaning that can transcend their strict definitions. However, don't take the suggested symbols as factual or literal. They are only an

119

attempt to explore the mystery. The list and the connections drawn are very personal to me and come from my culture, but they may not be universal. They may matter to me in one way but not to others in the same way. The goal is more to get you to think of your own interpretations rather than buying into mine. An example of how personal a word or idea can be comes from a childhood joy I experienced.

My father was a dear, sweet man who had a subtle yet delightful sense of humor. One day, when I was not quite yet a teenager, my father called me and my mother to look out the back kitchen window. It had snowed the night before, and there was a skim of white frosting covering our backyard. There, among the tangle of rosebush branches encased in that cold wrapping, bloomed a beautiful rose. My mother and I were enchanted and excited to see something so beautiful and so amazing. We had exhausted our expression of delight when my father began to laugh good-heartedly, confessing that it was a plastic rose he had placed there. Since then, when I see a flower of any kind appear in an unexpected place or circumstance, I take it as a message from my dear father. That is a personal image I enjoy, but it is not greatly shared or in any way universal that other people would think of my father were they to come upon that same image.

There is deeper meaning in so many words. The Divine speaks to us in symbols, metaphors, images, redundancy, and idioms. Has the Divine spoken to you through any significant words or symbols? Have there been words or symbols that seem to keep coming up in your life?

This language of the Divine creates something that withstands the test of time, sometimes for years, decades, even centuries. Much of Jesus's most profound and beloved

120

teachings were delivered in parables because they symbolized the truth of Divine nature, the Spirit among us, and the sacred within us. We look at the stories in our own culture that have withstood the test of time: nursery rhymes, fairy tales, universal mythology, epic journeys, and miracles. Many people hear them, and most come away with the same messages that people have been gaining from them for centuries.

Has anyone told you what was your first spoken word? At the time, speaking that word was a fabulous wonder, often celebrated and broadcast among circles of families and friends with great joy. There it is, that simple beginning of our gift of speech that eventually morphs into the written word, and then explodes into the beauty of poetry and prose, fantasy and history, commentary, and lyrics.

Do you think God lives in our words? You are beginning to recognize Divine presence when something repeats itself in our culture in many ways and many forms, even more if it crosses cultures, even more if it takes on double meanings or multiple meanings. So, what is in a word? Just a single word?

Choosing your own word is a way to create an anchor for yourself. We have discussed how a word can have many meanings—some universal and others quite personal. I encourage you to consider the spiritual practice of choosing a word that describes you, your spiritual journey, your relationship to the Divine, to which you can return when you find yourself lost and adrift. This could be a word that has power and presence (just like God being present) and one that might serve you as you seek to know God's presence through your life.

You might just find your word popping up everywhere—billboards, advertisements, speeches, things family or friends

121

Choosing your own word is a way to create an anchor for yourself.
(Photo by Robert Els for Quechua Benefit)

say to you, a word that springs from a book when you turn the page to a random place. You just never know, perhaps it may alert you to God's presence in your life, helping to point your way and guiding you as a companion on your path. I will share my word and other people's words with you here.

My word is **Enlightenment.** I embrace three interpretations of this word. The first is *Enlightenment as the Indwelling Spirit.* As discussed before in this book, in Quaker tradition, the word "Light" is used to represent the Divine, God, the Christ Spirit. To "hold one in the Light" is to hold that person in the presence of the Divine, which is a prayer for them that avoids telling God what you want for them. To seek the Light within is to know "that of God" within yourself, and to see the Light in people is to know "that of God" in them. Therefore, the Indwelling Spirit aspect of the word *enlightenment* speaks

PRESENCE *Recognizing the Divine in Your Everyday Life*

to the essential and eternal "in-Light" of people. The presence of the Light within can represent the soul, or possibly humanity and God combined.

The second interpretation is *Enlightenment as Insight.* To be enlightened is to be informed, which leads to understanding. My experience of enlightenment includes the revelation of the awareness, knowledge, and wisdom that come from Spirit, sometimes called insight. If you believe that there is that of God within, then you can tap that source by searching for knowledge that will help guide you and help with answering many of life's questions.

The third interpretation is *Enlightenment as Comfort.* God truly lightens; that is, the Spirit removes our heavy burdens and replaces them with Light. My relationship with God brings comfort and peace to my heart and soul. It is a condition of human existence to know pain and struggle, and yet relief from that, comfort through that, is available in the presence of the Spirit.

Looking at words chosen by several others, we can learn from them. In a class I teach that is based on this book, participants offer their thoughts. They volunteered these words within minutes of asking them to consider choosing a special word meaningful to them.

Inclusion. John chose the word *inclusion.* He said it came to him rather quickly and felt right. Coming from a childhood in which he felt "othered" by some of the neighborhood children, *inclusion* spoke to him, coming from a powerful and emotional wound. He is a person who believes in social justice as practiced by Jesus. John spoke of how Jesus included everyone in his ministry and went out of his way to minister specifically to the marginalized in his world, including those

123

who were poor, sick, and not welcomed. John went on to speak to how having a relationship with the Divine was like being included in the love of the Holy Energy, and that the partnership was inclusive.

Decorate. Rachel's word was *decorate.* She knew her word instantly because she had actually chosen it as a young child, but never really shared that with anyone. As a young girl, she liked the look of the letters and traced them over and over in cursive to see how attractive they were. As she grew, the word remained special to her. She likes the way it implies taking a space and enhancing it, making it special, and beautiful. It also implies the concept of a "do-over." Think of all the do-overs we get in life from God. How many times in the chapter about God's persistence and things that repeat did we talk about getting second chances?

To decorate also means to honor, recognize, and acknowledge, as when someone is decorated for valiant acts. Is that not what happens to us in our connection to the Spirit? We are acknowledged as we connect in that relationship with the Divine. The Bible speaks of God knowing the number of hairs on our head (see Luke 12:7). That's acknowledgment!

Mother. Janet's word was *mother.* She shared this in her written explanation: "I want to gather up all the little kids, teenagers, adults, and elders who are hurting, who are crying, in pictures, in newspaper articles, on the street, and save them, give them long, reassuring hugs, find out what the problem is, and try to make things right. Whenever I see little ones like that, my heart just aches for them. When I see articles on the psychology of parenting, I pay attention and read to the end. Through my identification as a mother, I watched that horrible video of George Floyd's murder, and what I saw was him as a

124

vulnerable child in great need. When I see people in difficult situations—of their own making or caused by others—all I see is the child they were and how frightened they must have been. Does that make any sense?

"Something about mothers being nurturing (and my own dear mother being a wonderful nurturer, sensitive to my moods, a great listener, and yet still holding the line when I was not on it) and being the symbol of what connects families, what allows us to nurse wounds of all types and helps us grow truly resonates with me. I can't let others just look miserable in a crowd or feel alone without trying to do something. Because that's where I was and I know how it felt, and sometimes all it takes is a kind word, interest, showing care, and a hug to help someone move on and find happiness or love or whatever it is they need."

What is your word? It may be something that comes to you instantly. Perhaps it is a word you have already been thinking about as you are reading. Or it may take some quiet reflection and some searching before it comes to you.

Your special word can give you a secure base from which to continue your search for the presence of the Divine. Do you notice the word in things you see, hear, and experience? When stuck on your spiritual path, does the word help you get unstuck? Give it a try and see what might fit for you. Remember to think of the symbolism of the word—what it evokes in your emotions, your heart, and your connection with the Divine.

Symbols survive over time, and we keep them because they speak to us from a common core, from some inward place beyond our limited mind. Because they evoke our innermost

125

essence, they stimulate that "still small voice"[2] temporarily beyond our hearing, but its quiet inner call beckons us to explore. These symbols maintain a hold on us. That is why we don't throw them away, and the ones that are most universally loved and treasured resonate the loudest, resulting in staying power. They speak to our condition, and we cling to them. They speak from our inner knowing (gMind) despite our devotion and attention to things external (iMind).

This kind of learning makes us be open, understanding that God may use words in ways that we do not. Perhaps Spirit speaks in a language almost foreign to us, and yet it still invites our understanding. If we embrace the idea that God speaks to us in multiple ways, we may discover that presence in our encounter with words wherever they appear.

Look to Genesis 11:1: Now the whole earth had one language and few words (RSV.) As with the Pentecost, languages were spoken so all could understand. Symbols allow

---

2 Quakers' founder, George Fox, found that becoming still and silent opened the connection between a person and the Divine to make possible hearing that still small voice. Because Quakers have faith in a direct connection to God without the need for an intermediary such as a pastor or priest, preparing oneself to hear and listen to that whisper is vital. Here is the Biblical reference: 1 Kings 19:11-12 New King James Version.

"God's Revelation to Elijah: Then He said, 'Go out and stand on the mountain before the Lord.' And Behold, the Lord passed by, and a great and strong wind tore into the mountains and broke the rocks in pieces before the Lord, but the Lord was not in the wind; and after the wind an earthquake, but the Lord was not in the earthquake; and after the earthquake a fire, but the Lord was not in the fire; and after the fire a still small voice."

those who do not speak the same language a way to interpret the deepest images in the language of God, though we must be prepared to hear and see in ways formerly unfamiliar to us, and we might find that we become used to having God communicate with us this way. Symbols connect us to the presence of the Divine.

As you reflect on this chapter, continue to ponder. Has the Divine spoken to you through any significant words or symbols? Have there been words or symbols that seem to keep coming up in your life? What does it mean for God to use words? Is it possible that the Divine will appear to you using words that only you recognize? Is it an act of faith for you that God will use words to get your attention? Are you going to begin looking for words that speak to your innermost longing for connection? Is this a way that you will finally hear?

"In the beginning was the Word."

Chapter 8
Metaphor for Deeper Meaning

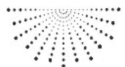

We will now continue to explore the power of symbolic meanings by extending beyond a word into the world of metaphors.

A metaphor is a figure of speech that is used to make a comparison between two things that are not alike but do have something in common. A metaphor can usually be made by stating something *is* something else, and metaphors are very expressive. It helps to explain an idea and it is not meant to be taken literally. Metaphors make a point in a more interesting way.

Some examples of metaphors are: She is an angel. Kisses are the flowers of affection. His temper was a volcano, ready to explode.

For our purposes, a metaphor can be an object or concept that describes something that has a deeper symbolic meaning than the word you chose in Chapter 7 that represents you. Consider how we explain the Divine. We have attempted a vague explanation by saying *God is a mystery* in Chapter 1, which is somewhat of a non-explanation.

Yet, because God is a mystery, metaphors become an ideal way to explain God and our relationship with God. When we say, "God is Love," which is often used as a way of describing God, is that a

A metaphor makes a comparison between two things that are not alike but do have something in common. (Photo by Robert Els for Quechua Benefit)

metaphor or a statement? You can search for a metaphor that will be symbolic of your spiritual philosophy, life philosophy, relationship with God, and/or life purpose.

Choosing your own metaphor is a way of expanding the symbolic framework of your life because metaphors are the language of symbols. The Bible, a book descriptive of God, is full of them. A metaphor can be representative or symbolic of something else, especially something abstract. It isn't literally true, but it helps explain an idea.

For example, a rock or mountain could be a metaphor for loyalty or steadfastness. A lighthouse is a powerful metaphor for having the inner Light (of the gMind), as a guiding Light for safe passage through life.

The Divine uses words and symbols in ways that we seldom do—as if it were a code. When we look back at the list of words from the previous chapter, some are associated with broad concepts, and therefore can lead us toward finding deeper meaning. Let's look at an interpretation full of symbols and

129

metaphors from the Bible and walk through some symbolic meanings that transcend the literal story.

The following is the story of Jesus walking on water and speaking to his disciples. Matthew 14:22-33 from the NRSV — New Revised Standard Version Bible:

> Immediately he made the disciples get into the boat and go on ahead to the other side, while he dismissed the crowds. And after he had dismissed the crowds, he went up the mountain by himself to pray. When evening came, he was there alone, but by this time the boat, battered by the waves, was far from the land, for the wind was against them. And early in the morning he came walking toward them on the sea. But when the disciples saw him walking on the sea, they were terrified, saying, "It is a ghost!" And they cried out in fear. But immediately Jesus spoke to them and said, "Take heart, it is I; do not be afraid."
>
> Peter answered him, "Lord, if it is you, command me to come to you on the water." He said, "Come." So Peter got out of the boat, started walking on the water, and came toward Jesus. But when he noticed the strong wind, he became frightened, and beginning to sink, he cried out, "Lord, save me!" Jesus immediately reached out his hand and caught him, saying to him, "You of little faith, why did you doubt?" When they got into the boat, the wind ceased. And those in the boat worshiped him, saying, "Truly you are the Son of God."

130

Let's explore some possible symbolic meaning of this story. Interpreting symbolic meaning takes some practice, and it isn't an exact science. However, we can consider some options.

Immediately he made all the disciples get into the boat. Modes of transportation represent being on a spiritual journey. This wasn't just a fishing boat. It was the spiritual journey the disciples were about to take.

... and go on ahead to the other side. The "other side" is often a way people speak of the spiritual realm. The disciples were about to go into a spiritual experience.

... while he dismissed the crowds. This spiritual lesson was only for the disciples, those who were willing to learn from his teachings. Those not willing to learn were not to be part of this journey/lesson.

And after he had dismissed the crowds, he went up the mountain. Placing oneself "higher" is considered closer to God. The top of the mountain is the place where Jesus can be closer to and one with the Divine.

... by himself to pray. One-on-one with God.

When evening came. The time of day is symbolic. Evening is the time of transition, for rest and reflection, separate from the time when goals are accomplished in the daytime.

... he was there alone, but by this time the boat, battered by the waves. The disciples' spiritual journey was losing direction and becoming in danger of weakening.

... was far from the land. Not able to be grounded, strong, or safe.

... for the wind was against them. They were not going with the breath of God, but against it.

131

And early in the morning. The beginning of another day, a possible time for getting important things done.

... he came walking toward them on the sea. The sea represents the gMind, the mind of God. By walking on the sea, Jesus was fully supported in God's strength, as if he were walking on land, because his relationship with God was whole.

But when the disciples saw him walking on the sea, they were terrified, saying, "It is a ghost!" Not a real person, someone from the "other side," the spiritual side.

And they cried out in fear. But immediately Jesus spoke to them and said, "Take heart, it is I; do not be afraid." The reference to heart also refers to love, which is considered the opposite of fear.

Peter answered him, "Lord, if it is you, command me to come to you on the water." He said, "Come." So Peter got out of the boat, started walking. Peter left one journey to go to another: from the boat, with the other disciples, to become one with the mind of God on the sea, as Jesus showed him to do.

... on the water, and came toward Jesus. But when he noticed the strong wind. This was the wind that was against them, that which was against the mind of God, making it from the iMind.

... he became frightened, and beginning to sink. He was no longer one with the mind of God.

... he cried out, "Lord, save me!" Jesus immediately reached out his hand and caught him, saying to him, "You of little faith, why did you doubt?" When they got into the boat. Back to his spiritual journey, but without achieving wholeness with the Divine.

132

... the wind ceased. The breath of Godly presence ending this experience or lesson.

And those in the boat worshiped him, saying, "Truly you are the Son of God." None of the disciples reached out to take the next step on their journey except Peter, and Peter tried and almost made it, but his doubt and fear kept him from full wholeness with God, even though Jesus was showing him that this was possible.

How powerful, indeed, are the metaphors in this passage. Perhaps, as a child, you read this Bible story and took it literally. You can explain it as fact by saying that walking on water is a miracle; however, there is also the possibility of rejecting the story as unbelievable when approached as factual, based on experience and observation. Someone may think that it is impossible to walk on water and not believe in the magic of miracles, and therefore reject the entire story.

When seen symbolically, with metaphor as the teacher, the meaning is far greater than the literal story. Now the story doesn't *have* to be factual to be able to hold truth. Because there is more mystery in metaphor than in fact. Symbols and metaphors more closely fit the concept *God is a mystery,* and they express the language of gMind.

I searched for a metaphor that described my relationship with the God of my understanding while I was at Loyola doing my graduate work in pastoral counseling. The result would express my spiritual, philosophical, and professional foundation from which I lived and worked. My Quaker spiritual teacher had introduced a concept several years before

133

that had struck me squarely in my gMind. Although he spoke of the concept only once, it had instantly become one of my favorite things, and I recognized its importance in my life immediately, reflecting on the concept we remember: *The Divine will appear to you in ways that only you recognize.*

My personal metaphor is the concept of an artistic phenomenon called *pentimento.* When an artist first paints on a new canvas, the resulting painting is not always what the artist wants to keep. Painters of old were often so poor that they could not afford to buy a new canvas for every painting, and so they often used a canvas that had already been painted but with a disappointing result, and they painted over the original painting. This custom was fairly common among many of the famous artists whose works now hang in museums.

Affected by the elements of time and light, the original painting can begin to show through in a ghostly way. This ghost is a *pentimento.* The word comes from the Italian word for repentance. Repentance is called for throughout the Bible as a summons to a personal, absolute, and ultimately unconditional surrender to the Divine. Though pentimento includes a sense of sorrow and regret, it is more than that. In repenting, one makes a complete change of direction toward God.

For me, the original painting represents *original blessing.* This is my belief, and opposite from the widely held concept of original sin. Original blessing is the spiritual gift we are given by God as a condition of our birth. There are no exceptions to this original blessing. Everyone gets it, and you don't have to do anything to receive it.

Some like to call this the grace of God. Because of the split in our spiritual condition, our choices can result in our pain and discouragement, or lead us to be unkind to ourselves and others. These choices form the layers upon our own canvas. Over time, many layers cover up our original painting, our original blessing, that is given in pure love by the Divine. Can you think of times in your life that created an overpainted picture on your canvas? That overpainting can contain image after image that discourages the revelation of the pentimento.

Though pentimento includes a sense of sorrow and regret, it is more than that.
(Photo by Robert Els for Quechua Benefit)

The layers of overpainting can become more transparent over time, allowing the first painting to show through. The tough work of self-examination, truth seeking, prayer, and encouragement helps our overpainting to become transparent. The force it takes to allow the pentimento of our being to become visible requires a partnership between the enlightenment of the Spirit and the persistence of the human soul. I have experienced a universal thinning of the overpainting as I become more aware of my own experience of enlightenment. This is also a way of recognizing how my word, *enlightment*, is connected to my metaphor.

Let's look at the example of my counseling client John from Chapter 7 and see how his word, *inclusive*, relates to his choice of metaphor. Remember, John saw great meaning in his word. He felt it spoke to his spiritual relationship with the Divine in how they were joined. It also represented his

135

philosophy of life, as he spoke about how inclusiveness was needed in the world to heal and strengthen people, ideas, and ways of life.

His metaphor was a Venn diagram, which is an illustration that uses circles (or sometimes other shapes) to show the relationships among things. Areas that overlap have a commonality while where they do not overlap do not share those traits. Venn diagrams visually represent the similarities and differences between two or more concepts. With the three-circle Venn diagram, the center of the diagram is created by an intersection of the three circles and forms a geometric shape known as a Reuleaux triangle—ABC in the diagram.

John chose the Venn diagram as his metaphor while reflecting on how some consider themselves *unrelated,* for example, human and God, genders, races, and cultures. However, John's spiritual and philosophical belief is that all *are* related. The Venn diagram allows for each aspect in a circle to express its individual and unique traits. However, the beauty of the diagram is in the connection of all the circles in the intersections.

It is when we connect with one another and with the Divine that we become whole. The Reuleaux triangle is the center, where there is the combination of all. When we as a people connect fully, we are most like God, our shared center.

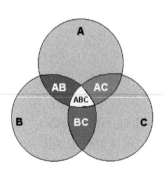

Venn Diagram

John also considered a different diagram in which humanity was a Venn diagram within one big circle, and that circle represented God, who was around everything.

"What is inside the circle is important," John said. "What overlaps is important, and what is outside the circles is important. The Venn diagram as my metaphor is a symbol that combines the spiritual and Earthly, and communicates conceptually, spiritually, and physically.

"I strive to find overlap with people, cultures, and my relationship with God," John continued. "The overlap includes ideas and shared vision with friends and my community. And the more I can find areas that overlap, the greater and deeper my happiness."

As you reflect on this chapter, continue to ponder. What metaphor speaks to you? Where are you in your spiritual journey and what have your struggles led you to seek as a metaphor that gives meaning and purpose to your personal relationship with the Divine? Take some time, and if something doesn't come up for you immediately, look at art, music, and literature for inspiration because *the creative arts invite us to touch the face of the Divine.* Can you pray for your answer? Can you accept that *God wants all good for you, God wants you to learn and grow, and the Spirit will lead you, guide you, push you, and open the way for you?*

Chapter 9
Nursery Rhymes from God

The treasures uncovered in this chapter (and those chapters that follow) will hopefully deepen our experience of recognizing the Divine in the stories of our culture and in our current lives. We will look first at how literature takes even the simplest words and weaves the Divine in the stories that have thrived generation after generation. Then we will explore the profound in the simplest literature, the poetry that produces nursery rhymes.

We have been discovering how we search for meaning (or deeper meaning) using language and symbols that transcend literal meaning. We paint word pictures by comparing things that are alike or not alike, by pushing together opposites, and by connecting multiple broad concepts. We do this in our thoughts, in our words, and especially in our stories.

How can we tell if a story echoes the language of God? Or if the Divine is speaking to our gMind through a story? Let's apply the concepts that our lives have been constantly filled with the presence of the Divine (a concept explored in Chapter 1) and that God will use all available means to get our attention (a concept developed in Chapter 3) as we look closer at the presence of the Divine in literary works we all know.

Clues that we explored in the earlier chapters help us identify literature as significant. Consider the persistence with which a body of literature has endured. Does it resonate, is it persistent, does it repeat? Does it teach? Has it become a favorite thing? Do you turn to it for influence, support, and rejoicing? These attributes mark the literature that has survived from long ago, including the Bible, and it also survives in some of the earliest literature we learn as children.

We explored the imagery of words in this book and discovered how powerful they can be. There was even more impact as we encountered metaphors, which convey deeper meaning.

If I say the word *green,* what comes to mind? Probably several images that you can expand on with some thoughtful images. If I say the metaphor "the green blanket of first spring," the meaning and symbols expand tremendously. Now we are stepping forward into an area of more complex literature. If we progress to the poem (song lyrics) of Kermit the Frog's "It Isn't Easy Being Green," we can discover the language of God as it flows into and through our spirit.

The overarching genre of poems covers so much. Poems can be the basis for nursery rhymes, song lyrics, commercial jingles, or a whole variety of verses. In this chapter, we will look at something we have all experienced when we were most open and innocent, what children for generations have delighted in and persisted in recalling: nursery rhymes. They are often the profound, enduring, and resonating language of God.

My Quaker (F)friend Barry Morley was moved so much by the experience described below that he believed it to be the groundwork that opened him up to much of his exploration of the language of God in his unpublished book. This is how he first became aware of the power of the Divine as expressed in literature, starting with the nursery rhyme "Mary Had a Little Lamb." His words that follow describe the moment of his awakening.

One day as I washed dishes and stared aimlessly out of my kitchen window, the language of God began to seep into my awareness. My mind, slightly out of focus, had gone into neutral. In the midst of this, I caught myself humming under my breath. "Where did *that* come from?" I asked myself as I put words to the famous tune:

Mary had a little lamb,

Its fleece was white as snow,

And everywhere that Mary went,

The lamb was sure to go.

I sang the words to myself a second time, then a third. (When a three [3] or reference to something occurring three times surfaces in a story, it alerts us to recognize it as a spiritual reference.) I wondered if I was supposed to be getting some kind of message. It felt like the kind of intuitive wake-up call we get when we are suddenly aware that it's time to leave for an almost forgotten appointment, or time to take the casserole out of the oven. "Am I supposed to do something with someone named Mary?" I

140

thought. "Is there a Mary's Little Lamb dish detergent I should be using? Should I include more lamb in my diet?"

This line of inquiry led nowhere, so I sang the words again. Then, in a sudden rush of insight, as if a window shade had been raised or a curtain in the theater had opened, I saw what I hadn't seen before. "Oh," I thought, "Mary *did* have a lamb. Mary had the Lamb of God. And its fleece, metaphorically speaking, *was* white as snow."

"This is silly," my rational mind said. (Rational minds have a way of doing that.) "A virtually meaningless children's song (and nursery rhyme) doesn't have implications beyond its literal meaning." But something in my intuition resonated louder than my rational mind argued.

Let's look at the part of the nursery rhyme that we know best and experience it with our mind for God (gMind) to release the symbols and metaphors and delve into the language of God. As we explore this, we are going to slow down our ways of looking at something we seemingly have always known. Consider you are gently and carefully stepping quietly and purposefully through this poem/song. Rest your literal mind. If you find a doubting or skeptical voice creeping in, consider inviting that skepticism to stand aside for the moment and allow yourself to think that anything is possible. Much of the interpretation to follow is in the language and imagery from the Christian tradition. If that is not a tradition that helps your inquiry, approach it as a literary exercise for the appreciation of metaphor.

141

Allow yourself to think that anything is possible.
(Photo by Katie Safley for Quechua Benefit)

Mary had a little lamb,

Its fleece was white as snow

And everywhere that Mary went,

The lamb was sure to go.

Mary. My (F)friend's intuitive interpretation may have been right. Mary could be the Virgin Mary of the New Testament of the Bible, or she might be the metaphorical Mary as a symbol of purity, openness, willingness to trust, whose nature is full of potential, like an innocent child. We can all become like a virgin in this metaphor and be with the lamb. Is it possible that we all have the seed of the Divine within us?

... had a little lamb. The lamb can certainly be Jesus, as he is often called the Lamb of God. And the lamb can be the spirit of that which is divine, the spirit which passes through all things. Lambs often evoke thoughts of the sacrificial lamb (like Jesus).

Its fleece was white as snow. A lamb is covered with fleece just as the Light of God surrounds us. Its whiteness is symbolic of purity and goodness, just as Jesus, just as a child. The fleece, especially when viewed with light (Light) behind it, glows as a halo.

142

And everywhere that Mary went, the lamb was sure to go.
The lamb is always close to Mary, always present, just as the Divine is always close to us. Its relationship and closeness to Mary is told to us with confidence as the lamb was sure to go everywhere that Mary went. How is the lamb like or not like the Holy Spirit you may have first learned about as a child?

> *It followed her to school one day,*
>
> *Which was against the rule,*
>
> *It made the children laugh and play*
>
> *To see a lamb at school.*

It followed her to school one day. School can be the symbol of the daily world we live in with all its chaos and other people and politics, injustices, and rules. It is where we are taught that reality is outside us, that our attention needs to be focused outward (not inward). We are not encouraged to go to the deep, quiet place where intuition lies.

Which was against the rule. Rules forbid having the lamb at school. This might symbolize not bringing the sacred (lamb) into the outward (secular/iMind) school where inner learning is not honored. The outward teacher would be against breaking this rule, even if doing so brings such joy to the children.

It made the children laugh and play To see a lamb at school. The children laughing and playing are, as children of God, in the present moment. They are feeling and expressing joy, fully in their gMind because they are with the lamb and Mary. They are no longer paying attention to the outer—the rules of the school and of the outer teacher.

> *And so the teacher turned it out,*
>
> *But still it lingered near,*

143

And waited patiently about,

Till Mary did appear.

And so the teacher turned it out. The teacher (this outer teacher) is the one of the world with all the rules, the iMind, who calls us away from the Spirit. One of the outward teacher's goals is separating us from our tranquil inner place, from our imaginative life, from our spiritual center. We have competing calls to pay attention to our iMind and the world that supports it, or to our gMind, our sacred center, and the inner reservoir of the Divine. The outer teacher *turned it out,* separated it from Mary, from the children who were experiencing such joy.

But still the lamb lingered near.
(Photo by Katie Safley for Quechua Benefit)

But still it lingered near. But even then, even when the lamb was turned out, still it lingered near. Just as when we turn out the Divine in our own lives, God stays near, so all we have to do is gently open ourselves to Divine presence to reconnect.

And waited patiently about. The lamb waited patiently about, just as the Divine is always patiently waiting for us. The lamb and Mary are fully connected, so of course it would wait for her to leave the school. The school is the secular, and Mary will always reconnect with the sacred lamb. Mary and the lamb

144

are inseparable. This is the metaphor's promise. No matter how long Mary and the children are required to stay in school, even though they succumb to the call to look outward, the metaphorical lamb lingers near, readily available, and always accessible to people who seek to drift inward.

Till Mary did appear. All that needed to happen was Mary appearing. She doesn't have to *do* anything. She just has to be present, just as all we have to do to connect with the God of our understanding is to be present.

"Why does the lamb love Mary so?"

The eager children cry.

"Why, Mary loves the lamb, you know."

The teacher did reply.

Why does the lamb love Mary so? The eager children cry. The truly important question comes, of course, from the children, just as during the Passover Seder, it is the child who asks, "How is this night different from all other nights?" Wisdom, in the language of God, often comes from the children. The love the lamb has for Mary and that Mary has for the lamb is fully connected to be whole. What a gift Mary has brought to school with her.

Why, Mary loves the lamb, you know. The teacher did reply. Who imparts the wisdom of knowing that Mary loves the lamb? The inner teacher. The inner teacher answers the question by affirming to the children (to Wisdom) by saying you know, as we have always known, the answer is *love*. The metaphorical Mary, lamb, and children are bound together in an inward reservoir where love is sensed more fully than in the outward world of noise, distrust, and broken promises.

145

This insight into "Mary Had a Little Lamb" has always been there, but it has not been fully realized. From a silly childhood nursery rhyme, which like the lamb, won't go away, we begin to sense something about ourselves that we might have overlooked. As we do, the process of gaining access to the deeper meaning of the language of God begins.

We identify this little rhyme as special partly because of how long it has endured (from generation to generation and still being taught), how often and pervasive it is in our everyday culture (references to it can be found in other writings, comedy routines, advertisements, and more), and how easily it can take on deeper meanings when exploring the greater meaning of words and metaphor.

In researching "Mary Had a Little Lamb," I found some information fascinating to me. The verse's known author, Sarah Josepha Hale, lived from 1788 to 1877. Yet the rhyme is rarely credited to her. She wrote prolifically, penning many poems and books, and she was a well-known, prominent activist of her time. She was adamantly opposed to slavery, favored the Union, and championed education for women. Yet her fame did not endure her more than 50 publications. And the original rhyme was slightly different and had additional verses that also have been mostly forgotten.

In the same year of Hale's death,1877, Thomas Edison selected the opening lines of "Mary's Lamb"—the original title— as the first speech ever recorded on his newly invented phonograph, out of all the words that he could have chosen. I find it so interesting that the adaptation of the rhyme presented in this book is what has endured, and that in the telling and retelling of this little story, the most spiritually meaningful version has lasted.

146

The children laughing and playing are, as children of God, in the present moment.
(Photo by Robert Els for Quechua Benefit)

Another nursery rhyme, coincidentally also often put to music to make a song (I wonder how coincidental that really is) is my personal favorite. It, too, meets the criteria for the language of God:

It has endured.

It can be found (cross-referenced) in many other writings.

It takes on deeper meaning easily.

You have heard it many times. I will write it here with a different way of phrasing that helps reveal the deeper meaning:

147

Row, row, row

Your boat

Gently

Down

The stream.

Merrily, merrily, merrily, merrily

Life is but a dream.

Row, row, row. Row is mentioned three times (there is that sacred 3 again) and speaks to moving forward in water—moving forward on your spiritual path, as the concept of water often refers to the Divine. (Recall in our look at the deeper meaning of words that bodies of water are often symbols of the mind of God.) Rowing is also something you can do for and by yourself.

Your boat. Any vehicle can be symbolic of being on a journey. A boat has even more significance because it is on a water (Godly) journey. The boat depends on being one with the water (God).

Gently. Gently, not harshly or with abundant effort, but naturally with the flow of the Divine.

Down. The direction is not against the flow but with the flow of the God energy that is surrounding you and also guiding you. If you have ever rowed with the current (as opposed to against it) you already know how very different the experience is. When you are with the current, you feel supported by the natural force that helps you along the way and makes it possible for you to arrive at your destination easily.

148

The stream. The stream is a body of water, which, like all metaphors of water, symbolizes the mind of God. In this case, the nature of a stream appeals to a sense of movement and heading toward a destination.

Merrily, merrily, merrily, merrily. Stated four times, this speaks to the emphasis being greater than the work of rowing, which was mentioned only three times. This key statement tells us specifically what the intention of our mindset and heart purpose is while on this journey. This speaks to the nature of the journey and the intent of the journeyer. It is pure gMind.

Life is but a dream. Here we are told specifically that this current physical world and life we live in is *not* our true world. This world is the dream, and our spiritual world is the reality. Though this material world can feel real to us, it is an interesting question to ponder if our human life or our soul life is our authentic state. Or are they both? One of my favorite questions is, "Are you a body with a soul? Or a soul with a body?"

In this simple child's verse, I find such profound wisdom and guidance that applies to life in a universal way. Both this rhyme and the rhyme "Mary Had a Little Lamb" are far more important than they appear at first glance.

Not every nursery rhyme rises to the level of the language of God. Many do not. The choice of a special nursery rhyme may depend on the person. What is meaningful for some may not be for others and vice versa. When searching for literary pieces that speak to you, let the literature find you as evidence of endurance and feeling. Just as with my (F)friend who became aware of a connection new to him as he was washing his dishes, so you may find your connection, like the lamb, by waiting.

149

Let the literature find you as evidence of endurance and feeling.
(Photo by Robert Els for Quechua Benefit)

As you reflect on this chapter, continue to ponder. Do you wonder why a child's poem, set to song, has been sung by generations? Can you see with clearer vision a deeper meaning in what was once so simple? Is it possible that God's loving and symbolic voice speaks to us in what we write and read that involves deeper meaning? Do you have something in your life, a phrase or saying, or perhaps something you or a family member repeat that can be considered more significant than on the surface? Could God be talking to us just as God spoke to many as described in numerous Bible stories?

PRESENCE *Recognizing the Divine in Your Everyday Life*

Chapter 10
Fairy Tales from God

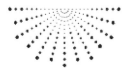

F airy tales, like nursery rhymes, are stories from our childhood. The best give us an understanding of human nature, fantasy, and moral lessons we need to carry into adulthood. They endure, just as nursery rhymes, because these stories resonate with a deeper lesson than sometimes seems obvious.

I imagine these are the lessons the Divine wants us to learn. That, in itself, gives us a clue that something is up with these fairy tales! When you get that subtle feeling that something is out of the ordinary, with profound meaning and powerful effect, you may be on to something that speaks to the language of God.

Let's look at what makes a fairy tale. Fairy tales are often traditional. Many were passed down from storyteller to storyteller before being written on paper. The protagonist of a fairy tale is never a superhero, a fairy, or a magical creature. Fairy stories are about someone ordinary, someone seemingly unimportant (like the son of a carpenter), who travels into an extraordinary realm full of wonder, magic, and fantastical beings.

Many family stories that your parents or grandparents may have told you off the top of their heads also qualify as fairy tales, in that many of the elements are made larger than life, or are omitted, leaving only those that seem directed by fate, chance, or strong character.

When I was very young, I had an elder uncle who didn't have the ends of all his fingers. When I asked him about his fingers, as a very young child would do without hesitation, he told me a story about a monkey nibbling the tips of his fingers. I remember him telling this story over and over. It was, indeed, a fanciful and memorable story in my childhood.

Many classical fairy tales are credited to no one author and may have been adapted and retold countless times. They exist in every culture in the world, and there are elements of the fairy tale going back as long as people have been telling stories. I have pondered if the fairy tales that have spanned generations also have a deeper meaning, related to our relationship with the Divine.

The elements found in fairy tales include the following[3]:

Special beginning and/or ending words: How many of your favorite fairy tales start with "Once upon a time" and end with "And they lived happily ever after?" Sometimes, there's a surprise ending. Some beginnings are actually timeless, as in God's time, not our time. Could the ending be a reference to

---

3 These categories appear on the website surfturk.com/mythology/fairy taleelements.html

PRESENCE *Recognizing the Divine in Your Everyday Life*

Fairytales are stories from our childhood.
(Photo by Katie Safley for Quechua Benefit)

our reconnection to the Divine, which results in eternal happiness?

Good character: Do you see a kind, innocent character? Is the good character clever? Is she or he helped by others? The connection between good and God (like the expression "Good God!") has always existed. The presence of a person of good character is symbolic of the spiritual goodness of God, the Holy Spirit, Jesus, the Virgin Mary, and other representatives of spiritual goodness.

This good character is sometimes represented by a plucky hero is often from a poor family, who for whatever reason goes off on an adventure and along the way encounters the evil character, giants, monsters, or dragons. By using her or his wits she is able to overcome them and thereby gain access to the treasure the monster is hoarding. She comes from the depths

153

of despair and poverty to fight the evil character. She brings the treasure home, and her family lives happily ever after. The plucky hero is our true self.

Evil character: Do you see a witch? A demon? An evil stepmother? A sinister gnome? Giants, monsters, and dragons? These are of the iMind, as they seek to keep us from the treasure.

In the end, the evil character usually loses somehow. Evil, though personified in fairy tales, can be understood as the absence of good, of God. When we are separated from our spiritual selves, when we turn away from the presence of the Divine in our lives, and when we embrace scarcity instead of abundance in the lives of ourselves and our fellow humans, we find that represented by an evil character.

Treasure: The treasure or goal that the main character is seeking is the gMind; it always represents God's unconditional love.

Royalty: Is there a castle? A prince? A princess? A king? A queen? We often symbolize the Divine as royalty because that is our Earthly experience of an ultimate leader. Given the dominance of the male-focused royal in our consciousness, it is common to refer to the kingdom of God, thy kingdom come, my lord and ruler, etc. There are countless references to a virgin, sometimes a young woman (princess), sometimes a virgin queen, who could possibly represent Mary. The prince in so many fairy tales, such as the prince in Snow White, can symbolize aspects of the Biblical Prince of Peace (Jesus). The prince brings embodied love, and he performs miracles, such as bringing Snow White back to life after a long sleeping death.

154

Poverty: Do you see a poor working girl? A poor family? A poor shepherd? Do you see poor people trying to eke out a living to have enough to eat? In the language of God, poverty often represents the poverty of spirit as in the Beatitudes: Blessed are the poor in spirit ("in spirit" appears only in Matthew) for theirs is the Kingdom of Heaven. The version in Luke focuses on the actual hardship, poverty, marginalization, and rejection of people who will see eventual vindication. Poverty is a spiritual state where we feel separated from God, or where we feel a lack of God's unconditional love. The key issue is that the literary portrayal of poverty symbolizes feeling separated from the Divine.

In fairy tales, as in the language of God, the poor can conquer their situations to become rich (symbolically connected to God and rewarded). Jesus saw people who were separated from the Divine as worthy because of their potential to connect with the love and grace of God.

Magic and enchantments: Do you see magical things happening? Do you see talking animals/objects? Could they remind us of Biblical miracles such as those directly from God (burning bush, parting of the Red Sea) and those performed by Jesus (turning water into wine, raising the dead, walking on water, making the blind see)? When you see magical things happen in fairy tales, in the language of God that means miracles and the presence of God in everyday life. Remember we are dealing with symbolism and metaphor.

So, an occurrence in fairy tales can point to a greater meaning that is spiritual, and may parallel, mimic, or reflect something in the Bible or similar spiritual writing.

Recurring patterns/numbers: Just as in an earlier chapter we considered the meaning of numbers in the Bible, they are

155

the same in fairy tales. They represent the conditions that are being described. "One" can symbolize unity and the Divine itself. Do you see any patterns? Often, you'll see things, phrases, tasks appear in "threes," "sevens," and "forties." Remember there are symbolic meanings attached to numbers that are often spiritual references.

Universal truths: The tale probably touches on some universal experiences (such as coming of age) or common hopes (to have enough food and enough love). Whenever we experience a universal truth, we are standing with the inner teacher of the Divine, where there are lessons and themes to help us understand the spiritual nature of our lives.

Let's look more deeply at a beloved fairytale, "Snow White." This was of particular importance in my (F)friend Barry Morley's life, as you will learn more about in the next chapter, as it played a significant part in his spiritual awakening.

(Note that images of white and black abound in this fairy tale, as they do in much of our literature. That humans have chosen to racialize these colors as shorthand terms for people originating primarily from two continents is both inaccurate and dehumanizing. I ask the reader to reject the notion of any implicit or explicit racial symbolism in the use of these descriptors.)

"Snow White" is one of those stories that everyone knows. The Brothers Grimm compiled this enduring fairy tale in Germany, publishing the first edition in 1812. Someone once

156

told my (F)friend, "Everything you need to know is in this story."

Walt Disney chose this story to make his company's first feature-length animated movie. It is the version of this story, depicted in that 1937 animation, we will look at now through our gMind. Doing so, we will find so much more meaning than is apparent on the surface. For our purpose here, we will take a look at a selection of words, symbols, songs, and metaphors that carry the language of God. I encourage you to view the movie to see so many more symbols for yourself.

As we are specifically looking at the version depicted in the Disney animation, the website Disneyplus.com helps tell the following story summary.

As the story unfolds:

In the beginning there was a good King and good Queen. At the beginning of the story, a queen sits sewing at an open window during a winter snowfall when she pricks her finger with her needle, causing three drops of red blood to drip onto the freshly fallen white snow on the black windowsill. Then, she says to herself, "How I wish that I had a daughter that had skin as white as snow, lips as red as blood, and hair as black as ebony." Sometime later, the queen gives birth to a baby daughter whom she names Snow White, but the queen dies after giving birth a short while later.

A year later, Snow White's father, the king, marries again. His new wife is very beautiful, but she is a vain and wicked woman who practices witchcraft. The new queen possesses a magic mirror, which she asks every morning, "Magic mirror on the wall, who is the fairest one of all?" The mirror always tells the queen that she is the fairest. The queen is always

157

When the queen asks her mirror, it tells her that Snow White is the fairest.
(Photo by Sonja Bales for Quechua Benefit)

pleased with that response because the magic mirror never lies. But when Snow White is seven years old, her fairness surpasses that of her stepmother. When the queen asks her mirror, it tells her that Snow White is the fairest.

When becoming aware of the language of God, in this or other tales and metaphors, we look at the same things we saw in the list of words in this book's Chapter 7: objects and things, people, animals, places, conditions, colors, numbers, and directions.

In just the beginning of the Snow White story, we find the following:

Numbers: three (drops of blood) and seven (the years it took for Snow White's fairness to exceed the stepmother's), both spiritually significant numbers.

Objects: the mirror, reflects the truth

People: stepmother (implied), the opposite of a true and loving mother/parent. This also represents the mind for the individual, the iMind, because she is obsessed with her looks and status and has little regard for the feelings of others. The stepmother/evil queen pursues Snow White (the fairest and most innocent gMind), trying to destroy her. Snow White, as a symbol of gMind, is the child of the true King and Queen, the beloved child of the Divine.

Colors: Snow White: her name is repetition, which adds emphasis. Snow is typically white, so her name means whitest of the white, purest of the pure. Snow White is to have skin white as snow (purity/gMind), lips as red as blood (full of life and mortal), and hair as black as ebony (the foreboding of evil). Note that these are also the same colors as, "... red blood to drip onto the freshly fallen white snow on the black windowsill." The repetition of the colors tells us to be mindful and pay attention.

Conditions: Death. Both the good queen and good king die, giving rise to the lack of goodness or God Presence in their child's (Snow White's) life.

Continuing on in the movie, we are introduced to Snow White as she is cleaning the steps of the castle, while white doves play around her. She then goes to the wishing well and brings up a bucket of water. At that moment, the prince appears on his white horse, and the prince and Snow White share a song. (If you can, use the Web or YouTube to watch this scene: https://www.youtube.com/watch?v=54QeNL5ih6A)

Conditions: Cleaning the entrance steps. Already we have an image of purity and spiritual humility (similar to Jesus washing the feet of the disciples).

Place: The steps to the castle. Home is symbolic of both heaven and of being one with the Divine. The steps are the steps on the journey toward that union, and the steps she is about to take on her spiritual journey.

Animals: White doves represent peace and purity surrounding her.

Objects: The well denotes the inner spiritual state and may imply yearning for something more; wishing is like praying. While you are sure you're addressing the Divine when praying, wishing doesn't call up that same listener. However, if God is everywhere all the time, would not God hear a wish? I wonder. The water is the symbol of the Divine, and the hauling of the bucket shows how she brings God from the well so she may drink of the spirit in communion.

People: The prince represents the Christ spirit, or the son of God. The prince arrives just as Snow White is at the wishing well (her inner spiritual state) and she is attracted to him immediately. At the end of the story, his kiss of "true love" and her union with him allow Snow White to rise from the dead.

Even before the prince arrives, Snow White, at the well, asks the doves who surround the rim of the well if they "want to know a secret." This reminds me of the concept God is a Mystery. Snow White says that if you send a wish into the well and it echoes back (things that repeat are a gift from God) it will come true. Just as she leans over the stone wall of the well, wishing for "the one I love to find me today," the prince on his white horse (purity parallel to that of the white doves) hears her and climbs over the stone wall to fulfill her wish (which may have been her prayer). Could both the stone wall of the well and that which the prince clears be meaningful?

Viewing the scene on the Web or YouTube is enchanting: https://www.youtube.com/watch?v=1Cfge09RERE .

Note that the lyrics of the song the prince sings also relate to a spiritual connection:

PRESENCE *Recognizing the Divine in Your Everyday Life*

Now that I've found you
Hear what I have to say!

One Song
I have but one song
One song
Only for you

One heart
Tenderly beating
Ever entreating
Constant and true

One love
That has possessed me
One love
Thrilling me through

One song
My heart keeps singing
Of one love
Only for you

Lyrics transcribed by Disneyclips.com

Both Snow White and the prince have been searching for the same thing, and each recognized it the moment they saw each other. Clearly the message in the song is the word *One*. The prince sings about one love, one song, constant and true. His song symbolizes the relationship of oneness or wholeness with the Divine.

The next part of the story develops as the evil queen calls the court huntsman and tells him to take Snow White into the

161

forest to pick wildflowers. There, he is to kill her and, for proof, bring back her heart. While in the woods, Snow White encounters a sad, crying bluebird (birds represent the spirit), foreshadowing the event about to take place. As the huntsman prepares to stab her, he falls to his knees (a position of prayer), kisses the hem of her skirt (as the Biblical woman does to receive healing from Jesus), and begs her forgiveness (as the Divine forgives us).

Her only way to save herself is to go into the unknown—the dark forest. (The dark forest represents the wilderness of the soul and starting the journey of transformation.) She eventually awakens to the light. (Note the time of day: dawn is the start of coming out of the darkness into the spiritual light.) She can now fully see the transformation of what once seemed to be ominous when in the dark. In the light, what were once scary creatures become sweet and loving animals (magical beings) who clearly adore her and now become her followers throughout the rest of the story (Disciples? Angels?). She speaks to them, "You don't know what I've been through all because I was afraid." (Fear refers to the separation from God as she encountered the dark forest.)

Snow White makes her way with the animals' guidance to the cottage of the seven dwarves. Along the way, they pass a river and waterfall (tributaries that flow into the mind of God, as all sources of water symbolize the Divine) and there are multiple references to the number seven, as the evil queen is later told where Snow White lives: "Over the seven jeweled hills, beyond the seventh wall, in the cottage of the seven dwarves."

Once in the cottage, Snow White begins cleaning—a condition of purification for the cottage, made of stone and

162

wood, symbolic of the Earth. Meanwhile, the dwarves work in a diamond mine (an inward place where treasure is kept hidden), which is dark, but lighted with lanterns to show the way out. The way into the mine is through a locked door, but the key hangs in plain sight right by the door. (Is the key to our treasure also in plain sight, but we keep the door locked? Is the key the gMind, and the locked door our iMind?)

As the dwarves discover and get to know Snow White, a number of symbolic events occur. She insists that they wash before eating. This speaks of ritualistic cleansing before consuming God's love, a meal prepared by her. The dwarves each have a special relationship with her. Dopey doesn't speak, and we learn that "words don't mean a thing" because it is what he *does* that counts. Her prayer asks that Grumpy will like her, hoping that he will connect with the love for things spiritual. She eventually kisses Grumpy, which transforms him, as God's love transforms us. For Grumpy, this is "love's first kiss."

Meanwhile, the queen-turned-witch (revealing her true nature) concocts a second plan to kill Snow White. She descends the steps in the castle, accompanied by rats, to brew an evil potion. (Contrast that with the opening scene of Snow White cleaning the ascending steps to the castle accompanied by white doves.) View this scene on the Web or YouTube and see the juxtaposition of this to Snow White on the steps https://www.youtube.com/watch?v=l9GJtM9lN-I.

As we all know, the murderous weapon fashioned is a poison apple (as in the apple of the Garden of Eden). Although the animals who love Snow White sense the danger that the old hag/witch/queen presents, they cannot save Snow White from taking the fatal bite. The animals summon the

163

dwarves, who chase the witch away to a cliff, where she falls to her death. She does not belong in high (spiritual) places.

The dwarves place Snow White in a glass-and-gold coffin (glass symbolizing being fully transparent, and gold symbolizing what is precious) and cannot "find it in their hearts to bury her" (she cannot go into the Earth). And so, the season goes into winter (a time of mourning when all things are still but not dead). Then in the spring, the prince, who has been searching for her the whole time (as God is always looking for us), places love's first kiss (God's love), which awakens her from "death" (transforming her separation from the Divine into connection with the Divine).

Snow White and the prince ride off together on a white horse (on a new spiritual journey), toward the castle (which might be seen as a symbol of God's mansion, kingdom of God), surrounded by the Light of God with happiness and joy (the true nature of the union of God and human), and live happily ever after (which is possible when united with God).

View this scene on the Web or YouTube to its end to see the Light beaming on Snow White as she sleeps and how the castle lights up as if in heaven: https://www.youtube.com/watch?v=pbdMHpoYo7Q.

Of course, there are many other fairy tales, and some also lend themselves more or less as metaphors for our relationship to the Divine. Snow White is the one that spoke to my (F)friend, yet there may be another that speaks to you. Your gMind, which clearly recognizes the language of God, can be applied to nursery rhymes, classic story lines, and fairy tales. Your experience of the Spirit will appear to you in ways that only you recognize, use others to teach you, and you may be supported by Divine influence. You may also find special

164

meaning in a favorite movie, book, song, or something that strikes you that you can't get out of your head. This becomes a constant that you love, which you never get tired of thinking about. As you open yourself up for searching, consider taking a lesson from the birds who are always seeking nourishment: God provides food for the birds, but doesn't throw it in the nest. Keep your search for meaning as a lifelong quest.

You may also find special meaning in a favorite movie, book, song, or something that strikes you that you can't get out of your head. This becomes a constant that you love, which you never get tired of thinking about.
(Photo by Katie Safley for Quechua Benefit)

We have been in the process of examining "Snow White" for its spiritual symbolism and looking at it through the lens of the language of God. We know that fairy tales are profoundly symbolic, magical, and mysterious. Once we have learned to do this, we can look at other forms of story that may not at first seem quite so symbolic as fairy tales. Family sayings, movies, and books may also be looked at through the same lens that searches for spiritual meaning in what at first appears to be not so spiritual.

After examining the complexities of the symbolism in this fairy tale, a class participant suddenly exclaimed, "Now I get my family's shared phrase we use for everything, 'When you take the low road, I take the high road.' The high road is the

165

road closer to God, and the low road is moving away from God."

I resonate with the movies *Groundhog Day* and *About Time*. Both are about do-overs, and they capture the spiritual journey so perfectly. God gives us so many opportunities to get it right.

A fairly recent reading of the book *One Good Mama Bone* by Bren McClain spoke to me of powerful spiritual metaphors, as it started and ended with a virgin birth, defined what it really meant to be a person of faith, and triumphed over death with resurrection, all while being a story about a cow.

Despite our skepticism, disclaimers, and sophistication, it is possible for us to recognize the Divine speaking in the written word—in long-loved nursery rhymes, fairy tales, poems, and all forms of story. It doesn't matter whether the great metaphors lie in lofty tales or simple rhymes. They maintain a hold on us. That is why we don't throw them away.

The ones that are most universally loved and treasured resonate the loudest. They speak to our (gMind) condition because they describe our condition. That is why we cling to them. They speak from the inner place, despite our devotion to things external.

As you reflect on this chapter, continue to ponder. Have you found yourself drawn to a story with a closeness that transends the ordinary? Is there a fairy tale that is especially meaningful? Would you now be able to look more deeply into the symbolism and imagery to find the touch of the Spirit in the words, images, and themes? Do you believe the Bible was written by God, or at least directed by God through humans? Do you believe this was the only time that the Divine has done

166

that? How reasonable or unreasonable does it seem that an ever-present God would still be sending us written messages and lessons?

Chapter 11
Waking Dreams

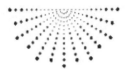

We have been talking about how God speaks to us in words, metaphors, poems, fairy tales, old sayings, the Bible, and other written works. God also speaks to us in dreams because dreams tap into our deepest reservoir in the language of God.

Here is where our real lives and imaginary thoughts, memories, and interpretations collide in fantasy. Emotions of supreme joy, loss, horror, and mystery come alive in vivid color and detail, all while we finally let our iMind, our mind for the individual, take a much-needed break. I wonder if our sleep state could be an Earthly experience that is similar to a spiritual state? Is it possible that our gMind, our mind for God, takes over in our dreams? If the Divine is always near, wouldn't that also extend to when we dream?

Many people find dream interpretation intriguing. When we sleep, and dream, we see symbols of all kinds. You might find yourself flying or encountering a monster. We almost expect there to be amazing or unusual symbols.

168

Our most memorable and significant sleeping dreams form a story that has a specific beginning and a specific ending (just like a fairy tale). We can sometimes remember these significant dreams all our lives, some of our dreams can repeat (and remember that repetition means to pay attention). Some are vivid and intense. They are all *meaningful.*

All the characters, whether in dreams or fairy tales, are aspects of ourselves. They reflect the individual aspects, or parts, of who we are and what we have experienced. Though fairy tales are external, and dreams are internal, consider how they may have some similarities. They both tell stories, they are steeped in symbolism, and those that are most significant evoke deep meaning to you and help you learn about yourself and others.

Barry Morley introduced me to an idea new to me. He believed that just as we have sleeping dreams, we are subjected to similar mysteries while we are awake. There are wakeful, real-life experiences that may also be experienced by others as they are happening. But they are remarkable to you, and you may carry the memory with you all your life. Upon recalling a wakeful, real-life experience with new eyes, you might find great symbolism and deeper meaning that magnifies the impact of your experience. These dream-like experiences that happen in your real life are called *waking dreams.*

It's as if the Divine is saying, "If you need some experiences beyond your sleeping dreams, I'm going to give you a waking dream." Remember, God will use all available means to get our attention. Have you told a story multiple times about an incident that was unusual, surprising, unique, maybe a little (or a lot) exceptional, or the height of coincidence? That may have been a waking dream. With your

169

Remarkable real-life experiences may stay with you all your life. (Photo by Robert Els for Quechua Benefit)

knowledge of mindfulness, symbolism, metaphor, and the ability to see deeply into story, you will begin to be able to recognize these when they happen to you or other people.

Certain events that happen in our waking lives have the language of God in them. They have many of the aspects of a sleeping dream, including symbols and metaphors with great significance. They have a specific beginning (almost like the opening, "once upon a time") and a specific end. Most importantly, they are meaningful.

Sometimes when recounting a waking dream to another person, if a third person were to overhear, not knowing you were talking about a real event, they may think you were talking about a sleeping dream.

Waking Dream: Barry Morley's Introduction to Snow White

Here is a real-life event that happened to Barry Morley. He was in a beach resort town on the East Coast. These are his words.

One day at a weeklong conference I attended, I went out at lunchtime to sit high on a grassy hill,

170

eat a sandwich, and gaze at the sea. What I received that day might not have been given to me had I not sat on that hill. The metaphor of looking outward over the sea may have made it possible for me to look into my inner portion of sea.

A man sat down beside me. It surprised me that he sat on the grass dressed in a freshly cleaned and pressed suit. "You mind if I eat my lunch with you?" He asked as he set his briefcase down between us.

"No. Go right ahead," I replied, disappointed that he had interrupted my sea gazing.

He opened his briefcase and took out a lunch that was so much more sumptuous than mine that I was jealous. Underneath lay a single book, a brightly illustrated, coffee-table version of *Snow White and the Seven Dwarfs.*

"Why are you carrying *that* in your briefcase?" I asked.

"Because everything you need to know is in there," he answered.

Let's uncover the symbols and metaphors in this *waking dream* that reveal the language of God.

One day at a weeklong conference. Week refers to the number seven, a spiritually significant number.

Lunchtime, eating a sandwich. A time to take God's sustenance, which often happens around meals.

171

Sit high on a grassy hill. High places put us closer to the Divine.

Gaze at the sea. The sea symbolizes the Divine. Barry Morley was contemplating and being with the mind of God, connecting with his gMind.

A man sat down beside me. Even with all the open space on that hill, this person was close to him, like the lamb and Mary in "Mary Had a Little Lamb."

It surprised me that he sat on the grass dressed in a freshly cleaned and pressed suit. This is significant. The suit makes the man appear not of this beachy, casual world where in the summer most everyone else was in shorts or a bathing suit. You get the idea it was highly unusual. The suit is also clean, which is a reference to the Spirit, and pressed, indicating perfection, free of the wrinkles that a worldly garment would have. And my (F)friend was *surprised.* Surprise is a wonderful condition that alerts us to God showing up!

"You mind if I eat my lunch with you?" The breaking of bread establishes a sacred bond.

He set his briefcase down between us. The briefcase is significant. It represents work that needs to be done. It is set between my (F)friend and the spiritual messenger, symbolizing work that needs to get done between them, work that connects them.

"No. Go right ahead" I replied, disappointed that he had interrupted my sea gazing. God will use whatever means possible to get your attention.

A lunch that was so much more sumptuous. This spiritual man was clearly expressing abundance.

172

A single book, a brightly illustrated coffee-table version of Snow White and the Seven Dwarfs. This book was attention-getting, and it contained a story that became a life-changing spiritual gift for my (F)friend.

"Because everything you need to know is in there." This was a message of both guidance and direction, indicating that this was what my (F)friend should focus on from that time forward.

This actually happened, and it had a profound impact on my (F)friend. It led him to the major work that he pursued for the rest of his life. He believed the fairy tale Snow White was a metaphor of the deepest spiritual meaning.

Let's look at this encounter another way and build some check points we can use to recognize this as a waking dream. There need to be five criteria:

1. A specific opening with a once-upon-a-time-type beginning

2. A specific story ending

3. Filled with metaphors and symbols

4. Aspects of the story are unusual, magical, bizarre, or inexplicable

5. If you overheard this story, it would sound just like a sleeping dream.

Waking Dream: The Prophetic Journey of Three Accidents

Let's look at another example of a waking dream. I experienced this when I was living on my farm, with my adult daughters and my young grandson.

One morning, my barn manager, John, told me a story about someone he knew who had been dishonest by stealing medical equipment meant to be supplies in a first responder facility. The person had made an excuse about the stolen medical rescue property, saying he might need it "if he were the first to arrive upon an accident." I had a very strong (stronger than what would have seemed appropriate) reaction to the thief making such a ridiculous explanation that was clearly a fabricated defense, and heard myself saying, "I have NEVER been the first to come upon a car accident in all the years that I have been driving." Although it didn't seem so significant then, later that evening, my comment would have an eerie echo.

Later that evening, after the bad weather had kept us in all day, my two adult daughters, my grandson, Christian, and I decided to go out to dinner. There was pea-soup thick fog, it was dark, and the condition of the roads was unknown because the approaching colder temperature might make the road surfaces freeze, making them slippery at any moment, so I was driving far more slowly than usual along a very long road. While we were distracted with idle talk, I thought I saw something ahead, but was, at first, unsure. I eventually realized in the foggy, dark distance up ahead that there was a car stopped in the middle of the road resting perpendicular to me. Yes, the angle of my car to the stopped car was a "T" and I was

174

on the road in a legal lane, going straight. Once I became fully aware of it, I immediately started to brake and kept saying, "Oh God, Oh God, Oh God ..." as I was concerned about my ability to get my car to stop quickly and safely on a road that could be slippery. If I couldn't stop, I would T-bone this strange car sitting in the dark by itself on the road.

I *was* able to stop, just barely, with inches to spare, and with no slipping, and no problem. As I looked into the mirror, I saw a car coming up behind us, and again was afraid that it might not be able to stop because they now had to see my car at a complete stop sitting without apparent reason in the midst of a long dark stretch of the road. But that car stopped without trouble as well. The other cars that eventually came up from behind were all able to stop.

We soon realized we were the first car at the scene of an accident coming from our direction. The accident had happened right in front of us, but none of my family had seen anything or heard anything because of the dark, the fog, and the distraction of our conversation.

We could now see three vehicles had been involved in an accident, and all were completely still. At first, we saw no movement. One vehicle, to our left, was a truck with a snowplow. The plow was crushed into the front of the truck as if it had been made of aluminum foil. I was amazed that the impact of the crash had crushed something as substantial as a snowplow.

Soon I noticed that the driver was visible and moving. Someone from the opposite direction had walked to the truck and was standing at its door. The car that had caused us to stop was upright and exactly in the middle of the dividing line, perpendicular to the road. A third car was off the road to our

175

right, in a shallow ditch, upside down. My daughters and I ran out of our car. One daughter went to the car blocking us and the other to the overturned car, while I went to the truck. My one daughter asked if we should call 911, and I agreed.

I approached the truck and heard the standing man speaking to the driver. Then we both were asking the driver if he was all right. He seemed only semiconscious and had blood coming from his head.

It was then that I realized with both my daughters and me tending to the accident victims that no one was with Christian, strapped into his car seat, back in our own car. Because there was someone helping with the driver of the truck, I decided to go back to my car to check on Christian, anticipating that the four-year-old would be panicking and crying. When I got into the car, he was perfectly all right. I stayed with him for a while as more people appeared to help those in the three cars.

The person at the truck ripped open the driver's door, which was now hanging by a thread, but still blocking the driver's ability to get out. He helped the driver get out, unsteady on his feet, though he began taking some steps on his own.

It was still foggy and dark, so I couldn't see much going on with the other two cars. Eventually, fire trucks and ambulances arrived, and they began applying the jaws of life on the upside-down car on the right. My daughters returned, and we determined there was nothing more we could do.

I simply made a U-turn and headed back up the road to take a detour to the restaurant. Driving away, I realized that had I been going the speed limit and arrived at the spot just seconds earlier, we might have been in that same accident. For

176

me, it was a "pay-attention" event because I had just spoken aloud those words that morning about never having been the first to arrive at a car accident.

Let's look at the symbols and metaphors that may be present in this waking dream.

"I have NEVER been the first to come upon a car accident in all the years that I have been driving." This was a prediction/prophesy. Things can happen for the first time, even though they may never have happened before. They get your attention that way. They can also pave the way for what is about to come.

Driving in the car. Being in a vehicle represents your spiritual journey. The direction of this journey was moving toward sustenance (eating/food): All of the cars in the accident represented journeys stopped.

Going slowly. My reduced speed (a good pace for my gMind) and calling God helped me focus and got me to that place that had been foretold earlier in the day.

On the way to a meal. Meals and food in general stand for receiving Divine substance. Going to a meal is a metaphor for preparing oneself to be filled.

Dark and foggy. Conditions surrounding us were unclear, not seeing, heading toward something that is uncertain, possibly foreboding, and suggesting something hidden. I was very aware that I looked and looked again before seeing what was right in front of me—like we often have the Divine in front of us, but cannot see clearly because of our personal darkness and fog.

An accident had happened right in front of us, but we didn't see it. The main event in this waking dream was about

177

accidents: Anticipate that things are going to happen in your life that are out of your control and are often a metaphor for the uncertainty of life. Some things are just not the way they are supposed to be. Sometimes things are right in front of you, but you can't see them.

Three (3): A number with spiritual significance. My daughters and I are three adults. There were three vehicles in the accident. I called God three times.

"Oh God, Oh God Oh God": I found myself calling out to God.

Stopping: The other car (spiritual journey again) in the middle of the road, stopped, forming a "T" with me because it was perpendicular. I was just able to stop safely, barely inches away from it. Perhaps the message in this includes: Wake up, Mary, this is about spiritual journeys, and what can happen when accidents happen. This has crossed my path and made me stop like the proverbial brick wall. (Cross? Jesus' cross?) There was also some focus on the other cars that came behind me once I stopped. They all stopped safely.

People are hurt and in danger. Their journeys (their lives?) have been disrupted, and I am there, first on the scene to see it and offer help, so are my daughters.

The need I felt to go back to the car (back to my journey) and be with Christian. Could Chris represent the Christ within my journey? And he is just fine, in contrast with the hurt, danger, and chaos all around.

Jaws of life (breath of life?) on the right. In literature, the right side represents the spiritual side. There is a successful rescue saving the journey and journeyer. That car in the

178

accident was upside down (not right-side up—not as it should be).

U-turn. Literally, "you turn." To continue on my journey to get to sustenance, I have to turn around and go in a different direction. I still have the Christ within my car who is safe, and I can leave this accident behind. Those directly involved are safe, in part because we had been there and called for rescue and help for them. Note, this is also the end of the story/dream.

We can see that this real-life waking dream meets the criteria we have set forth: A specific opening with a once-upon-a-time-type beginning, a specific story ending, metaphors and symbols, aspects that are unusual, magical, bizarre, or inexplicable, and if you overheard this story, it would sound just like a sleeping dream.

Why even pay attention to waking dreams? Because they are meaningful. How was this meaningful to me? Here is what was going on in my life at the time.

Sadly, although my 10-year marriage had begun with hope for a long and happy relationship, it had been failing for many years. I stayed with the hope that it would improve, but it wasn't going well. This waking dream spoke to me of how things were unfolding in my life.

I can only attempt to interpret below, but I welcome anything you may see that I have missed. You might want to identify the words, symbols, and metaphors you read that parallel the actual events of that night.

Like the man who stole and then lied about the rescue equipment, my marriage was taking so much goodness away from my life. I stayed on that long, slow dark road where there

179

was no clear way for my journey to improve. Only through calling God to help and the presence of my daughters could I find a different way, and though fraught with much dread and danger, I had to stop this journey I was on.

As sad and dangerous as it was to end my marriage, I was faced with a number of choices. I could let this heartbreaking life change and crush me forever, or it could turn my life upside down, or I could just put an end to it—a time out—and look to the Christ within for calm, love, and reassurance even though I couldn't see beyond that for any reassurances for a good future. Overall, I needed to have a goal to fill myself with the presence and strength the Divine would provide, trust that the nourishment of my soul and that of my dear girls' and grandson's lives would be present and would give comfort. Ultimately turning away from the relationship had become the only thing to do. My girls and Chris would be with me, though I would have to leave so very much behind. And I would be headed in another direction in my life, which would be filled with Divine sustenance.

Sometimes a waking dream presents itself with a wealth of symbolism and a lifelong memory even though it may appear at first as a fairly simple random occurrence. When stories surface that are powerful for people, I think of my friend Rosalyn's story that she considers special.

Waking Dream: The Cemetery in Halifax, Nova Scotia

Having a passion for all things Titanic, Rosalyn longed to visit the graves of the people lost on that fateful ship's journey. The cemetery is in Halifax, Nova Scotia. She remembers reading about the tragic ship sinking, which started her search. Here is a summary of her story.

> I can't talk about it without being emotionally moved, but for 40-some years I had wanted to visit this place. About three summers ago, I drove to Halifax and hired, through TripAdvisor, a guide, Paul. Though the cemetery was the #1 tourist attraction and hundreds of people from tour buses are there daily, when we arrived, there was only one other vehicle there. We were able to see so much more than if among the usual tourists. Paul showed us where someone had hidden a coin in the monument to one of the victims. During my time there, I felt touched and moved, and felt that the circumstances were very special for me (not having anyone else around at a usually crowded place). That visit was a highlight.

Emotionally moved. In addition to being a waking dream, this experience reflects the impact of recognizing a Divine event that perhaps only you experience as special. Look at the effect reflected in this humble story. Rosalyn speaks of being emotionally moved even when talking about it in the present moment, and she felt the circumstances were very special, and she felt touched by the special circumstances (by the Divine?).

Numbers one, forty, and three. Spiritually significant numbers are present in the story.

Paul. The guide was named Paul, who was the great storyteller of Jesus's life and mission.

Recognize a Divine event that perhaps only you experience as special.
(Photo by Katie Safley for Quechua Benefit)

The *hidden coin* is symbolic of sacred treasure, something of value, reminding us to pay attention.

Highlight. Finally, Rosalyn ends the story by describing the event as a highlight. Things that are high are closer to the Divine, and we know already about how the word *light* speaks to the sacred.

It is also noteworthy that what drew Rosalyn to have passion for those lost in the sinking of the *Titanic* departed in the great mind of God—the sea.

Waking dreams can be found in many of the often-told stories of your life or the lives of your family and friends. Some of the stories in this book are waking dreams, and now that you can recognize them, you can probably find them.

PRESENCE *Recognizing the Divine in Your Everyday Life*

Remember the woman at the gas station who encountered the angry man? They were both in their vehicles, there to refuel, both on their journeys and in need of a message in their shared experiences with one another.

Waking Dream: The First Day of Writing PRESENCE

We have also had another waking dream brought to our attention in this book. When you first read this story in Chapter 1, you wouldn't have been able to recognize it as a waking dream, but now you can return to how the journey of this book began and recognize the language of God speaking through the words and story.

The beach can be enlightening. This day was no different, with a calm breeze, the lapping of bay waves, and still-warm sand. As Summer and Fall struggled to decide what temperature to be, and with only a few people to be seen, I walked slowly at the water's edge that morning with my beloved shaggy terrier, Pixie, running ahead. Someone in the distance, who was slower than I, greeted Pixie who had nosed her way into the solo walk of the stranger.

The woman, about 40ish and pretty, had that beachy casual style of not needing to care about looks. She turned as I attempted to keep my dog from being a nuisance. All was clearly in good stead when we made the expected greeting as two people on a morning beach walk often do, with smiles and a sharing of how lovely all of it was.

She carried a plastic bag with her, partially filled with something I couldn't see, and she clearly was searching for something in the sand. She told me that about a year before,

183

after many years of strolling on this beach, she had found the handle to a trunk or drawer that was intriguing in its age and look, and had taken it to the local museum for identification. She learned that a merchant ship had sunk not far into the bay sometime in the 1700s. No one remembered it being there for centuries. Then, a few decades ago a boat began dredging the area. Its heavy digging device literally shattered the Maria Johanna, the Dutch merchant ship, unintentionally destroying what had previously laid sleeping and untouched. Glass windows were smashed, and the cargo of liquor bottles was destroyed.

Now, after many years, the glass still washes up on shore, particularly when a low tide leaves the path of shells, stones, and sea animal remains in the wavy line that parallels the water's edge. The broken glass, now smooth for the bathing of the waves and sand, washes up with the rest of nature.

Having found the handle, and learning of this story from the local museum, the beach comber began a search for something that had been there all along, the glass pieces from the bottles and windows, but until now had not been in her awareness. She showed me how to recognize them on the sand, how they proved to be glass when holding them up to the light of the sun, and how to tell the difference between the window glass and the bottle glass. Showing me the plastic grocery bag with that day's found pieces in it, she said, "I come to the shore now about three times a week and continue to search for the glass. I have thousands of pieces I've collected. It is my passion to collect these. It still amazes me that something that has been here my whole life just became present in my life last year, and now I see it easily, and it gives me such joy and purpose to find it." This collector learned to recognize the glass treasurers from the sea through her new-

184

found awareness and focus, as well as her new knowledge, and in this pursuit she found a sense of purpose.

She brings a second bag to collect trash and garbage left on the beach to keep it clean. That simple act, so easy to add to her passion of glass collecting, protects the birds and other marine life that might mistake plastic for food.

We walked together for a while as I looked at the glass pieces she collected that day and I learned how to recognize them. After a while, I felt it was time to part, so Pixie and I turned around toward the direction from which we had come. The woman and I spoke pleasant goodbye words and shared smiles before I stopped and turned back. I felt that I should have asked her name, but somehow it didn't happen and I felt the loss of a missed opportunity.

Within just a minute, as I walked back, I passed another person, and again, introduced by Pixie's greeting, began to have idle chat. Having missed the opportunity to ask my glass-collector her name, I made sure I wouldn't do that again, and when I asked this second person what her name was, she responded, "Mary." I was surprised to hear my own name, Mary, spoken aloud.

Let's look at the symbols and metaphors that may be present in this waking dream.

In the beginning was the word. It is worth noting the timing of this waking dream. This was officially the first day I was to put pen to paper and begin writing this book. I had no plan of how to write the start of the book despite decades of experience, study, and mentorship that would lead to its

185

content. That this happened day one, hour one, of this most momentous day sets this waking dream apart from the ordinary. In this experience, as in most circumstances, I only became aware that it was a waking dream upon reflection. I am rarely aware that something is a waking dream in real time as it is occurring.

Slow pace at the water's edge. The sea symbolizes the mind of God, and here I was going slowly (as when I was driving slowly in the dream involving the three accidents) and connected to the Divine represented by the edge of the water, which also reminds me of the Footprints story.

The woman was at a distance. It seems that this tends to set the stage for waking dreams for me. As in seeing the car from a distance in my other dream, I saw the woman, at first, from some distance. She was even slower than I. Each of us was alone, just one, on our own journeys, connected by the Beloved, then we were two, together.

Spiritual numbers are throughout the story. The woman's age appeared to be about 40. 1700 being the time the woman said the ship sank. (The one and seven have significance.) She came to the beach 3 times a week to search.

She was seeking. Her story was also meaningful. This wasn't just a random walk she was on. She was looking for something. It was purposeful. Only one year before she found a handle—perhaps to open her own journey. Whenever I come upon a word that resonates, I play with it. Did she need to get a handle on her journey? Was the handle there to open up something? This handle led her to her eventual quest for the glass. As she told the history of the ship, she mentioned the name of it, calling my attention to it since it was a combination of mine and my first daughter's names.

186

The Maria Johanna. This treasure chest lay sleeping deep in the sea, the mind of God, until its treasure was released by the dredging. Often our own treasure doesn't emerge from deep within without a strong force to release the treasure or awake us to its presence.

The glass. The glass was the treasure. The sunken treasure. Remember, treasure symbolizes the Divine. Like the sea glass, often our own inner treasure is sometimes transformed from trash to treasure by life experiences, hard knocks, time, and motion. She was searching for the Divine. It had always been there. She said she had been coming to the beach for a long time, but not until she found the handle did it lead her to learn of the glass. Although always there, she had never been aware of it. She taught me how to recognize the different kinds of glass on the sand, how they proved to be glass when holding them up to the light of the sun, and how to tell the difference between the window glass and the bottle glass. So, was she teaching me how to find and recognize the treasure? The Divine? Her own story was a waking dream inside my waking dream, and she taught me how to search for and recognize the glass, recognize the Divine. This became part of the title of my yet unnamed book. She taught me to recognize the Divine, the treasure, that had always been there but for looking for it. And how did she show me how to tell if, indeed it was the true treasure? Why by holding it up to the Light. And when she spoke of her own journey, she defined it. It was her passion. She used that word, passion.

The second woman. Why was the second woman, separate from the first, in the dream? Of all names, her name was Mary, my name. I heard my own name called aloud, asking me to pay attention. Could this second meeting have been that second chance we need in our lives so often? Realizing my

187

shortcoming in not naming the first woman, I was given another chance.

Pixie. I haven't forgotten one of the central figures in this waking dream. My dog (you do know that dog is god spelled backwards?) She was the reason for my taking the walk, she caused me to meet the first woman, and the second woman. Would a pixie have been sent to connect three women on a special day? Our beloved pets are so often our comfort and our guides.

I was the third woman. There is the completion of the sacred three. I went out on my journey, paid attention, learned from the teacher, and returned to write my life's passion. From this waking dream came the book title, the premise that gave the book life, breath, and meaning. From this dream came the beginning.

All through the Bible, people talk about "an angel came and told me ..." What if way back in the Bible times, these people were having waking dreams? They could have had these profound, message-laden experiences. When they spoke of them to others, perhaps to their children and grandchildren, they conveyed the meaning as well as the actions. People often did not read or write, and their lives were rich with oral traditions.

What if they felt the spiritual connection in their waking dreams, and when they began telling others, especially children, over and over, they said, "One day an angel came to visit me, and this is what happened ..."

188

I wonder how far your observations of your own life can be stretched.
(Photo by Dale Cantwell for Quechua Benefit)

Can you look at your life as it has unfolded and remember a time, an incident, perhaps only a few minutes in length, that has always stayed with you? That incident will stand out to you because it has had meaning and purpose far beyond what you would ordinarily expect.

Write the story down, just as it happened. Then go back and see what words, symbols, and metaphors surface that give it a deeper-than-surface meaning for you.

The Divine is right here with us. When it is time for us to search for something that has always been there, it will be there, perhaps in a waking dream. You won't forget it, it will always be with you, filling your sacred center, for the Divine always has PRESENCE.

189

As you reflect on this chapter, continue to ponder. How far can your observations of your own life be stretched? What if your waking dreams are coming from such a spiritual source that it feels like an angel (a messenger from the Divine) wants you to discover it because it will be vital on your spiritual journey?

Chapter 12
Next Steps on Your Journey

Don't miss the chance to know God better. We might miss a million things if we don't recognize, reflect, and go deeper. Consider asking this important question in your life, "If not constantly present, if not in our daily experiences, then where is God in all of this?"

Consider carefully what you can carefully consider. Ponder. Wonder. Ask. Open up. Be curious.

In John Milton's Sonnet 19, written as he became completely blind in approximately 1652, he stated if we stay in place, the angels still disrupt our complacency by changing the things around us, "they [angels] also serve who only stand and wait."[4] So even if I stand as motionless as I possibly can either through will or by chance, I am, in fact, spiraling though space on planet Earth. We are always traveling, moving forward,

---

4 Milton, John, "Sonnet XIX When I Consider…" *Complete Poems and Major Poems*, edited by Merritt Y. Hughes (New York: Odyssey Press, 1957) p. 168

PRESENCE *Recognizing the Divine in Your Everyday Life*

even when we feel most held in place or stuck. We are always on our journey. In that same sonnet, Milton also reveals his spiritual understanding of how we best accept God's presence, "who best bear his mild yoke, they serve him best."

Moving forward: Even when we feel most held in place or stuck, we are always moving forward.
(Photo by Katie Safley for Quechua Benefit)

Milton implies that the acceptance of the presence of the Divine is gentle and easy.

While we may increase our energy and focus, hoping to achieve that next step on our spiritual journey, the paradox for me has been that some of my most progressive times have been through the experience of stillness and silence. Surprisingly to me, the hard work, frustration, and all-out *trying* to get further on my spiritual path needed only to be replaced with mindful contemplation and a sense of ease.

The unanswered questions continue.

Any number of subjects not explored in this book may be worth considering as you continue your journey. They will certainly come up as you walk your path. Here are but a few.

Heaven, Hell, and sin are full of meaning and controversy among people who pay attention to their spirituality. They are certainly worth exploring as you formulate your unanswerable questions about life and the realm of the Divine.

192

Our gMind reminds us how to live in a way that is connected to the Divine and to each other.
(Photo by Robert Els for Quechua Benefit)

Angels are mentioned 273 times in the Bible. That's a lot of mentions for a subject we seldom consider. For people who study such things, angels seem to be organized in a hierarchy, have names, and some are fully described in the way they look, think, act, and carry out their mission. Have you considered the role angels play in your everyday life?

Going to church (or not) is a loaded issue. Choosing a church in my experience was a formidable adventure. I have a suggestion as you approach this consideration: Be drawn to where they place more energy in asking questions rather than in giving you answers. I am fundamentally driven by the concept that God is a mystery. Therefore, I like being among other people who seek continual revelation rather than choosing to close down all options but one. Watch not what they say, but what they do, to determine their true belief.

193

Christianity, at least the forms it takes in the present-day United States, is complicated. The question I find especially complex is, "Are you a Christian?" because the answer depends on the questioner's definition.

I treasure Jesus's life story, his lessons given through parables, his teachings, and what he did according to the written words in the New Testament. I find his lessons simply truthful and enduring. I embrace that Jesus was inclusive, not exclusive. He showed us how to live with all our neighbors, and he taught us not to hold ourselves above others.

I grew up with this tradition, and I embrace the beauty and the mystery. However, I also wonder about what my professor, a Catholic nun, told me about her view of Christianity in my last class in pastoral counseling at Loyola of Maryland. She said that for her, Christianity was not *the* answer, it was *an* answer.

There is plenty for spiritual people to do. Racism is basically hate. Discrimination against women, LGBTQIA+, and religions other than your own is basically hate. Failure to help the poor, the food insecure, and those who suffer is basically hate. Meanness to one another for any reason is basically hate. How do you change the hate?

I wish I could eliminate all hate, and yet sometimes I can barely take care of my own mundane existence. Therefore, I can only do what I can to be a little better every day. I reconnect with my mind for God, having sacred faith that our gMind reminds us how to live in a way that is connected not only to the Divine, but to each other.

If only we can become aware. If only we can recognize the Divine in our everyday lives.

194

Reflect and Ponder

At times, I have sought to depend on any clue of wisdom in time-worn expressions such as *in God's time not your time*, or *for everything there is a season*, or some song, lyric, poem, or catchphrase, while hoping and yearning for a spiritual sign to bring me enlightenment. There are times (that seem like eons) when it appears as though nothing is happening toward my spiritual growth, no matter how hard I think, talk, pray, read, or pay attention.

Sometimes when we use the word *journey*, we imply there is a destination. I wonder, though, if the point of our lives is that we have already arrived through Original Blessing? Waking dreams, sleeping dreams, favorite things, all we have mentioned here in PRESENCE and more could be Spirit's way of saying "know that I am with you." Notice every day and see how everyday things can be sacred reminders that beauty, peace, love, and joy are with you at any moment because we are meant to enjoy each moment.

In hard times, having patience and gentleness with oneself opens you to Spirit's available love, tenderness, and comfort. God is urging us to seek and find peace and connection. Divine presence leads us through the fire to the cool water on the other side.

In closing, I pray for peace and love both for you—and for all. I return to the traditional King James Bible, as I leave you with my favorite psalm, the 23rd. If the Lord is the shepherd, we all are the lamb, and the last line sums up what we all have. We just need to constantly be reminded that indeed the Divine is in our everyday lives.

195

23 The LORD is my shepherd; I shall not want.

²He maketh me to lie down in green pastures: he leadeth me beside the still waters.

³He restoreth my soul: he leadeth me in the paths of righteousness for his name's sake.

⁴Yea, though I walk through the valley of the shadow of death, I will fear no evil: for thou art with me; thy rod and thy staff they comfort me.

⁵Thou preparest a table before me in the presence of mine enemies: thou anointest my head with oil; my cup runneth over.

⁶Surely goodness and mercy shall follow me all the days of my life: and I will dwell in the house of the LORD forever.

My spiritual journey has had times of great growth and powerful leadings. It has also had times of stagnation, resulting in an immovable, seemingly irreparable disconnection from my relationship with the Divine. Yet, what might appear as stagnation has a at times actually been an opportunity for stillness, when I have eventually become closer to Spirit.
(Photo by Robert Els for Quechua Benefit)

PRESENCE *Recognizing the Divine in Your Everyday Life*

As you reflect on this chapter, continue to ponder. How have the concepts and new perspectives in **PRESENCE** fit together for you? Remember the suggestion for you to absorb new thoughts and explorations as a dry sponge soaking up the clear water? How has that happened for you? Have you taken your time to ponder the unfamiliar? Have you taken pleasure in not knowing and in accepting that something can simply be a mystery? Have you gotten lost? Have you been found? Have you begun to wander off a path you were at one time so very sure about? Have you recognized the Divine in your everyday life?

A Tribute to Quechua Benefit

A surprising way that God has been present in my life has been the constant, repeated, central place Peru has had in my life and my heart. I have been to Peru eight times for various reasons, and I am considering a return trip. My children are of Quechua heritage, and they were born in Peru. The Quechua (pronounced "catch-oo-ah") are the native Peruvian people from whom the Incas rose as rulers before being annihilated by Europeans in pursuit of silver and gold.

Of all the animals I could have chosen to raise once I moved from the Washington, D.C., area to a Maryland farm, I chose full Peruvian alpacas. It was through my many years as

Help them any way you can.
(Photo by Robert Els for Quechua Benefit)

198

an alpaca owner and breeder that I came to know Mike Safley, founder of the dearest charity to me, Quechua Benefit.

I know Mike personally and have traveled with him to the Peruvian highlands. I know without question of the integrity and moral compass with which he guides this charity. Every penny donated goes directly to helping the poorest of the poor in the highlands of Peru.

Recently, St. Paul's United Church of Christ in Westminster, Maryland, has adopted the tiny, 800-person town of Ichupampa in the Peruvian highlands. The church has made available face masks and soap to all in the town, hoping to ease the devastation that COVID-19 has had on the mostly elderly population. The church is also subsidizing the midday meal for the poor elderly and assisting in the creation of a future Women and Children's Community Center. The Community Center will be built above the current kitchen that provides those meals to the town's residents who are food insecure.

Quechua Benefit focuses mainly on education and health but directs its various missions to the greatest needs as defined by the Quechua people living there. They have established a school for grades K-12 that operates on three campuses. *Casa Chapi*, serves the young children of the Colca Valley, the region of the famous rising condors. I admire what Quechua Benefit does, so I give my time and money to them to help. Their story can be found at www.quechuabenefit.org if you would like to explore what they do and help them any way you can.

PRESENCE *Recognizing the Divine in Your Everyday Life*

(Photo by Robert Els for Quechua Benefit)

PRESENCE *Recognizing the Divine in Your Everyday Life*

Concepts

PRESENCE *Recognizing the Divine in Your Everyday Life*

Chapter 1: Looking for Something

God is a mystery.

The Divine will appear to you in ways that only you recognize.

Your life is constantly filled with the presence of the Divine.

God speaks to us in a mysterious language that we can learn.

Chapter 2: Favorite Things

God wants all good for you.

God wants us to learn and grow.

The Divine wants us to enjoy our bodies.

The creative arts invite us to touch the face of the Divine.

Connecting with nature unites us with the Divine.

The Spirit will lead you, guide you, push you, and open the way for you.

Chapter 3: Divine Persistence

Repeated lessons are a gift from God.

Repetition with Divine resonance becomes tradition.

Persistence is one of the many ways the Divine reveals itself.

God will use all available means to get our attention.

God's persistence is present even when we are unaware.

Chapter 4: Events Large and Small

God will use others to teach you.

God will use you to teach others a Divine message.

God will enter your life as a teacher.

Chapter 5: Simple Plans

Your plan may be supported or derailed by Divine influence.

Divine influence is with you in the painful times.

God does not cause bad things to happen but comforts when they do.

The Spirit does not cause good things to happen but rejoices when they do.

www.PresenceEveryday.com

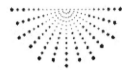

© Mary G. Jackson, MEd, MS, LCPC

The author grants permission to copy and share these Concepts pages.

CPSIA information can be obtained
at www.ICGtesting.com
Printed in the USA
BVHW091042140922
646847BV00002B/4